Dear First Lady

Also Available

Dear Mr. President:
Letters to the Oval Office from the Files of the National Archives

LETTERS TO THE WHITE HOUSE

★★★★★★ FROM THE COLLECTIONS OF THE ★★★★★★★

LIBRARY OF CONGRESS & NATIONAL ARCHIVES

Dear First Lady

DWIGHT YOUNG

and

MARGARET JOHNSON

NATIONAL GEOGRAPHIC

WASHINGTON, D.C.

CONTENTS

Helen Thomas

THE Driskill AUSTIN, TEXAS

Oct. 28, 1965

Dear Mrs. Johnson:

Thank you so much for the pen commemorating the beautification bill.

I was thrilled to receive it and your very kind note.

You did a great job in alerting the American people to the need for more beauty in their lives.

I hope this doesn't stop our traveling, now that the bill has been wrapped up.

Thank you again for your many kindesses.

Sincerely,
Helen Thomas

FOREWORD

Helen Thomas

REPORTERS WALK A FINE LINE when covering the White House: We do not want to be accused of cozying up to the First Family; neither do we want to be co-opted by them. We soon learn where we stand with presidential families—behind the eight ball. We can be seen as intrusive or insensitive, and First Families often believe that we are dedicated to exposing their failings or accentuating the negative. ✻ I always felt it was important to cover the First Ladies in the White House.

They humanized the picture, as did their children. In earlier times, reporters were much closer to the First Ladies. They gave regular interviews to wire services. First Ladies were often more frank than their husbands and would tell you more about the highs and lows of life in the White House. Occasionally, they would let their hair down and tell you what they really thought.

Much of that candid nature is reflected here in their letters. Each piece of correspondence gives a personal view of these unsung heroines while campaigning for women's rights or their husband's seat in office or while defending their husband's decisions of state or their own personal conduct. I had the privilege of knowing these remarkable women, and their voices here recall my wide-ranging and fascinating experiences while covering the First Ladies.

I was invited to my first White House Christmas party during the Roosevelt era, but I did not start covering Presidents day to day until the beginning of the Kennedy era. As a White House correspondent, I was invited to state dinners by most of the

Presidents and their wives. In that setting reporters are guests and do not carry notebooks, which always makes our hosts more comfortable.

One of my first personal interactions with a First Lady was with Mamie Eisenhower in October 1959. She was a charming, impeccable mistress of the White House and won the hearts of the people as the wife of a war hero who had liberated Europe. But, like Bess Truman, she never stole the limelight. At the time, she had been in the White House for more than six and a half years, and I was the president of the Women's National Press Club. The club, founded in 1919 as the women's equivalent of the National Press Club and the Gridiron Club (which excluded women), was celebrating its 40th anniversary. The First Lady, who was a big supporter of ours, agreed to move up her 63rd birthday, which fell on November 14, to make the luncheon a double celebration.

The first First Lady I covered as a White House correspondent was Jacqueline Kennedy, who had exquisite taste. Beginning in 1961, she embarked on extensive renovations of the second-floor family

suite and the formal state rooms, returning the Executive Mansion to its colonial-
era elegance. It's a tribute to "Jackie" that
she saw the beauty of the White House and
understood the significance of the history. She also successfully fought efforts
to tear down the old magnificent War and
State Department building, next door to
the White House, saying it reminded her
of the Opera House in Paris. Preservation
of the nation's great landmarks (including
Grand Central Station in New York after
she left the White House) will surely go
down as her great legacy.

Lady Bird Johnson was the epitome
of the modern First Lady, who recognized her duties and fulfilled them. She
understood the observation of Muriel
Humphrey, wife of the Vice President in
the Johnson era, that a First Lady could
wave a magic wand. She knew that if she
evinced an interest in any good cause the
world would beat a path to her door and
try to help her achieve her goal. She ral-
lied the nation, for instance, behind her
national beautification program to eliminate the giant billboards and auto grave-
yards along highways. In doing so, she
single-handedly made us more aware of
the grandeur of America.

I distinctly remember traveling across
the country with Lady Bird Johnson during the 1964 campaign on a whistle-stop
train through the South for four gruel-
ing, seemingly nonstop days. We in the
press felt that she understood us. At the
end of the beautification tours, her press
secretary, Liz Carpenter—a veritable P. T.
Barnum who could sell you the Brooklyn
Bridge—would haul out the champagne
and fried chicken for the hungry press
corps. That endeared Lady Bird and Liz
to us, I'll admit.

Pat Nixon understood the role and
played it well. She was very active and
traveled around the world as her husband's diplomatic emissary, a hit everywhere she went. But she also relied on her
old friends to visit from California every
once in a while to remind her of the freer
life she once had.

Pat brought relief supplies to volcano-
devastated Peru. She also visited several
needy countries in Africa and accompanied her husband on his breakthrough
trip to China in 1972. She was a warm
welcoming hostess to a revolving door of
visiting delegations, and more astound-
ing, she tried to personally answer every
letter sent to her at the White House.

Pat once gave a luncheon in my honor
at the White House after my engagement
to AP White House correspondent Doug-
las Cornell was announced. I considered
Pat a friend. I had covered her since her
husband was a senator, and I admired her.
Because of our friendship, it was especially tough to put questions to her during
the unraveling of the Watergate scandal.
Incredibly, she fielded them with poise
even though she knew there was no way
to save the Presidency. I remember when
we asked Mrs. Nixon if she would want
either of her daughters, Julie and Tricia,
to marry a politician, she said, "I would
feel sorry for them." But you married one,
we countered. "Yes," she said, "but I don't
tell you everything."

I regret that I did not get to tell her
how much I admired her and how beloved
she was despite the tragic ending of the
Nixons' political lives.

Betty Ford was her own person, fearless
and with refreshing candor. Unlike some
First Ladies, she did not try to hide her
real self. She wasn't afraid to say she had

been divorced before she married Gerald H. Ford, an aspiring politician from Grand Rapids, Michigan. Such personal revelations were not exactly politically expedient. She also spoke of having seen a psychiatrist and had a problem with drugs and alcohol, so sure that everyone would understand and take it all in stride, as she did many of her vicissitudes.

Rosalynn Carter was a companion to her husband in the White House and a soul mate. He treasured her advice and even set a precedent by having his wife attend Cabinet meetings, causing some consternation. Her major contribution was in the field of mental health. She became an expert in promoting better treatment of the mentally afflicted, and she testified before Congress on the subject. Her testimony helped get a law on the books for better care of people with

psychological problems. She was a real trouper and a terrific campaigner, but more bitter than President Carter when he was defeated for reelection.

When I covered the 1980 presidential election campaign, I interviewed Nancy Reagan and asked her what her "First Lady Project" in the White House would be if her husband became President. She replied, "I am just going to take care of Ronnie." I looked at her in astonishment and told her that he would have a raft of staffers taking care of him, along with the Secret Service around the clock. "You will regret not taking advantage of your tremendous opportunity and power," I told her.

A year later, Mrs. Reagan, looking like a beautifully dressed Rodeo Drive matron, caught a lot of critical notices from detractors who likened her to Marie Antoinette.

Mamie Eisenhower celebrates her 63rd birthday at the Women's National Press Club with club president Helen Thomas.

She soon turned that image around by taking up the cause of drug abuse among youth. As a result she became "Nancy" to the country, with her mantra "Just Say No" becoming a household catchphrase. She later told me that I was right and said that I had given her good advice about the honor of being a First Lady and the good things she could accomplish.

Barbara Bush seemed happy at first living in the White House. I remember interviewing her soon after she moved in and she said: "Now I can see George." President Bush had previously held many government posts, especially in diplomacy, that kept him away from home. There was no pretense about Mrs. Bush, who brushed off questions about her wardrobe and other personal inquiries, and said: "What you see is what you get." She adored her dog Millie and wrote a book about her. She was open to the press, but during the 1992 campaign when her husband was defeated for reelection, she blamed his loss on the media.

Hillary Clinton did not seem to enjoy the role of First Lady. She clearly preferred to be a close adviser rather than a socialite. President Clinton gave her a prime assignment at the start of his first term in 1993, to develop a universal health care plan, but she botched the project by keeping its details away from the media and Congress.

She learned a lot of painful lessons during her years in the White House, which served her well when she ran for the U.S. Senate in New York. As First Lady, however, she was distant to reporters, refusing to give interviews and seeking the pressroom space for her own staff. She had to attend the pro forma political and press dinners, but none of this was her cup of tea. It's my hunch that she would find the White House a far more satisfying post if she were to become the first woman President of the United States.

The last First Lady, Laura Bush, was a teacher and a librarian in her native Texas. Naturally, pushing education became her main goal in the White House, along with women's health issues. Although she protested she did not want to make speeches, she turned out to be an outstanding campaigner for her husband in his two successful runs for the Presidency. She has traveled to many countries in Africa and the Middle East as the President's emissary. But she has also kept up with all her old friends in Midland, Texas, and has vacationed with them, regularly taking time out from the White House.

All of the First Ladies in modern times rose to the occasion in their fashion. I have admired them all, knowing that so much is expected of them.

The book you are about to read is another great contribution the National Geographic Society has made to preserving American history. The First Ladies have been unsung heroines. They have been praised and criticized, honored and ridiculed, by foes and fans. But somehow they have been able to take it all in stride.

Each First Lady has realized that she has had a unique opportunity for her life and we have had great expectations for her. I hope this book will give a greater appreciation of the First Lady's role, especially among young people who are in need of her special kind of inspiration and vision.

Laura Bush is the ninth First Lady that Helen Thomas has covered as a White House correspondent.

INTRODUCTION

Dwight Young

ANYONE WHO WANTS TO KNOW what it means to be First Lady should ponder these statements by three former holders of the title. ❧ The first comes from Lady Bird Johnson: "The Constitution of the United States does not mention the First Lady. She is elected by one man only. The statute books assign her no duties, and yet, when she gets the job, a podium is there if she cares to use it." ❧ The second was made by Pat Nixon as she was walking with her successor, Betty Ford, toward

the helicopter that would take the Nixons away from the White House and into seclusion: "Well, Betty, you'll see many of these red carpets, and you'll get so that you hate 'em."

The third statement—wordless but eloquent—was made by Julia Grant: She sobbed upon leaving the White House at the end of her husband's term as President, because her eight years as First Lady had been the happiest of her life.

My guess is that if you gathered all of them in a room, from Martha Washington to Laura Bush, and asked them what it's like to be thrust onto the public stage as the wife of the most powerful man in the world, their answers would echo and amplify the statements of Mesdames Johnson, Nixon, and Grant: It's an opportunity, a burden, a joy.

It's also *tough*. Historian Lewis L. Gould has written, "Being a first lady . . . requires a woman to act, if she would succeed, as a mixture of queen, club woman, and starlet." It's more than an eminently quotable throwaway line; it's a

perceptive summary of the enormous diversity of roles the President's wife is expected to play.

So what does a First Lady actually *do*? What, exactly, is her job?

For one thing, she has to keep the home fires burning. First Lady Hillary Rodham Clinton may have insisted that she was "not some Tammy Wynette standing by my man," but many of her predecessors felt that their primary duty was to be a good helpmate to their husbands.

Martha Washington and Mamie Eisenhower, who had followed their husbands through years of military service, strove to maintain the home as a well-ordered sanctuary where the President could relax and forget—at least for a while—the pressures and awesome responsibilities that shaped his workday. Even Jackie Kennedy, not exactly the typical stay-at-home wifey, acknowledged that her husband didn't want to talk politics when he came home, hinting that an important part of her job was to divert and entertain him. Moreover, Teddy Roosevelt's

Betty Ford gazes toward the Oval Office from a window in the White House residence, January 20, 1975.

comment about his willful daughter—"I can be President of the United States, or I can control Alice. I cannot possibly do both."—is a pointed reminder that the mother, even when she is First Lady of the land, is traditionally expected to care for the children so their father can worry about other things.

In addition to being a homemaker, the President's wife should also be a confidante and touchstone who will listen to his ideas and help him figure out whether they make sense—someone like Bess Truman, for example, who made sure that her husband's policies and actions remained firmly rooted in the traditional values with which both of them had been raised. She has to be a loving companion, too—someone like Edith Galt, who, shortly before she married President Woodrow Wilson, was told by him, "I am absolutely dependent on intimate love for the right and free and most effective use of my powers and I know by experience . . . what it costs my work to do without it."

It's not easy being a wife, of course, and it's safe to assume that it's even less easy being the wife of the President—but when it works as it's supposed to, it's a beautiful thing to behold. Jerry Ford joked that his wife's outspokenness had cost him the 1976 election, but when he got laryngitis and couldn't deliver his concession speech, he asked Betty, not the chairman of his reelection campaign or a member of his Cabinet, to do it for him. He looked on lovingly while she spoke, and when she finished they walked away hand-in-hand.

The Fords' closeness illustrates another word that figures prominently in a First Lady's job description: partner. More than one First Lady has reflected on her White House experience by saying something like, "Well, when we were President . . . ." It's not a slip of the tongue, but a fact: For four or eight years, the President and his wife share what amounts, more or less, to a common career. Sometimes they constitute such an effective and inseparable team that they offer the electorate two Chief Executives for the price of one, though they'd never describe themselves that way, and most people would be outraged if they did.

Domestic policy adviser Stuart Eizenstat described Jimmy Carter's relationship with his wife, Rosalynn, by observing, "The Carters don't have friends, they have each other." The same comment might be made about many other presidential couples. John Adams, possessor of one of the brightest minds of his era, considered his wife, Abigail, his intellectual equal; throughout their long life together, he sought her views on a wide range of issues, and even when he neglected to ask her, she didn't hesitate to let him know what she thought.

Jimmy Carter often sent position papers and internal memoranda to his wife with the penciled question "What do you think?" Woodrow Wilson took things a step further, sharing state papers with his wife-to-be and even teaching her the secret code he used to communicate with foreign emissaries. Franklin Roosevelt didn't usher Eleanor into the innermost sanctum of power, but she functioned as his partner nonetheless: She traveled where he couldn't; saw and heard things that security guards and yes-men hid from him; and flooded him with so much information and so many opinions that he reportedly limited her to three memos a day. His reliance on her

was illuminated at the 1940 Democratic Convention, where the delegates were restive and unhappy with FDR's choice of Henry Wallace as his Vice President; unable, or unwilling, to attend the meeting in person, Roosevelt asked his wife to go for him, and her presence turned things around.

Rosalynn Carter once justified her practice of sitting in on Cabinet meetings—something no First Lady had done before—by insisting, "There's no way I could discuss things with Jimmy in an intelligent way if I didn't attend cabinet meetings." Having been her husband's partner in the peanut business and the governor's mansion, she fully intended to maintain their close working relationship in the White House, and that was fine with the President, who valued her insight and advice above anyone else's.

Whether or not she functions as a full partner, the President's wife is expected to be a valuable political asset to her husband and his administration. When he was asked for advice on how to win an election, Richard Nixon replied, "First pick the right wife. [She] has an enormous impact in bringing the man to people that the candidate is unable to reach." He was not the first or last President to realize that a savvy, personable, and willing spouse can open doors that might be closed to him, both on the campaign trail and in the White House. When Eleanor Roosevelt made history by holding regular

President and Mrs. Polk pose with James Buchanan and Dolley Madison, among others, ca. 1846–1847.

press conferences for female reporters, for example, she tapped into a previously undervalued media market and made a host of new friends for the administration—all by doing something her husband could not.

Being pretty doesn't hurt. The famously taciturn Calvin Coolidge, who looked, as some wag remarked, "like he'd been weaned on a pickle," married a woman who was everything he was not: attractive (Howard Chandler Christy's luminous depiction of her in a red dress and flowing scarf is the most engaging First Lady portrait in the White House collection), outgoing, and cheerful. Even though he occasionally felt obliged to rein her in, he undoubtedly realized how much he benefited by sharing some of the glow of his wife's popularity.

Noting how his wife's beauty and charm had dazzled reporters and heads of state alike on a visit to Europe in 1961, President Kennedy joked, "I am the man who accompanied Jacqueline Kennedy to Paris, and I have enjoyed it." Later, on a trip to India that drew admiring crowds and wall-to-wall press coverage, the First Lady said to a friend, "Jack is always so proud of me when I do things like this." He had every reason to be proud: She personified the aura of glamour and youthfulness—"vigah," the President called it—that transformed his administration into Camelot and drew a generation of young people into political activism.

Of course, the life of a presidential spouse isn't all pomp and pageantry, the huge Christmas tree in the East Room and the Marine Band playing "Hail to the Chief." Sometimes the friendly applause turns into a thunderstorm, with the First Lady in the unwelcome and dangerous role of lightning rod.

When she drew flak for assuming too great a public role in her husband's administration, Rosalynn Carter shrugged it off with "I had learned from more than a decade of political life that I was going to be criticized no matter what I did, so I might as well be criticized for something I wanted to do." It's a sentiment that might well have been echoed by many other First Ladies who took heat for a wide variety of offenses, serious and petty, real and imagined.

People whispered that Mary Todd Lincoln was hysterical, maybe even crazy, and possibly a traitor to boot. Nancy Reagan spent too much money on dresses and china. Hillary Clinton was too pushy, and Florence Harding was a domineering shrew. Betty Ford talked too much. Martha Washington put on airs, and so did Jackie Kennedy. Eleanor Roosevelt, almost certainly the most vilified First Lady of modern times, was blamed for just about everything that happened, from having the effrontery to write her own syndicated newspaper column to fomenting racial unrest.

Each of them must have endured dark nights of frustration and despair and even rage. Eventually, they all had to learn the same hard lesson: Sure it hurts, but it comes with the territory.

Some of them—the strongest—survived the bad times, or even drew additional strength from them, to win respect in their chosen fields of interest and eventually establish themselves as stars in their own right.

Grace Coolidge overlooks the National Mall, with the Washington Monument visible in the background, ca. 1928.

Not long after her husband died, Eleanor Roosevelt was spotted on a subway in New York, and an admiring crowd quickly gathered around her. She later told a friend, "It made me feel so good that people remember Franklin!" In fact, it wasn't the memory of FDR that sparked warm acclamation from the subway riders, it was Eleanor herself, who had set a new standard for First Lady activism. As former presidential speech writer Peggy Noonan noted in a recent *Wall Street Journal* article, "First ladies were once more or less average, and were expected to be. Now they are accomplished, worldly, and expected to be." It was Eleanor Roosevelt, with her gift for seeming to be everywhere and involved in everything, who made the difference.

Jackie Kennedy wasn't an Eleanor-style crusader, but she became a quiet arbiter of taste and culture in everything from fashion to antiques and French cuisine. It's often said of Lady Bird Johnson that she lived for Lyndon, but she carved out a niche for herself, too, as a champion of conservation and—even though she disliked the word—beautification. Hillary Rodham Clinton has already broken precedent by becoming the first First Lady to win elective office, and later, as a candidate for the job her husband formerly held, she was poised to shatter even more formidable barriers.

As Noonan observed in her article, "Candidates for the first lady's job have to find a balance. It's delicate. Strong is good, aggressive not. A person who cares, yes; a person who pushes an agenda, no." Given the thin line between boldness and "ladylike" demureness that the public expects the President's wife to walk, it's a wonder that any woman would want the job. Happily, plenty of women *have* wanted it, or at least they've accepted it with grace when it was presented to them, and the nation is better for all they've done and said and been. The members of the sorority of First Ladies are—there's no other word for it—an amazing group. Pick an adjective to describe them—talented, spunky, underappreciated, funny, courageous, tragic, smart, lovable, inspiring—and whatever it is, it fits.

Of the 39 women who were married to Presidents between 1789 and 2007, 30 appear in these pages. The numbers require some explanation. Five Presidents—Jefferson, Jackson, Van Buren, Buchanan, and Arthur—did not have a wife when they took office. Only one of them, Buchanan, never married; the others were widowers. Each of them chose a female relative or the wife of a friend or Cabinet member to serve as his official hostess, and while the title of First Lady is traditionally bestowed on these women, only one of them, Harriet Lane, is represented here. Woodrow Wilson remarried in office and so is represented by two First Ladies.

That leaves nine First Ladies whose correspondence does not appear in these pages. One of them, Anna Harrison, whose husband died of pneumonia one month after taking office, was First Lady for such a short time that she never had a chance to set foot in the White House. The others—Elizabeth Monroe, Louisa Adams, Letitia and Julia Tyler, Sarah Polk, Margaret Taylor, Abigail Fillmore, and Lucy Hayes—are missing for various reasons: Little of their correspondence has survived, their personal papers are not available for publication, or there simply wasn't room to include everyone.

Richard Nixon once said of himself and LBJ, "Both of us were very fortunate that we married above ourselves." Looking back at what the First Ladies have meant to us and given to us, it's hard not to conclude that we are the fortunate ones, lucky to have had them around for the past 220 years. The correspondence in this book offers no more than a glimpse of the issues they had to deal with, the wit and wisdom they dispensed, the joys and tragedies they endured, and the exuberant diversity of the women themselves. The letters are so wonderfully varied that it's impossible to generalize about them, except to say this: They are us.

Written on kitchen tables and executive desks, composed in anger and joy and confusion, they hold up a mirror that reflects the face of the nation in all its ingenious, heartbreaking, wacky, infuriating, inspiring, indomitable Americanness.

Whether we find the reflection flattering or appalling, it's worth a long, thoughtful look. ❧

Lady Bird Johnson, Patricia Nixon, Nancy Reagan, Barbara Bush, Rosalynn Carter, and Betty Ford gather in November 1991.

Madam   London October 7th 1796.

    I have desired Mr Anthony to present to you a proof Print
engraved from the whole length Portrait of the President, which
you may remember I painted in Philadelphia: ___ I beg
you will do me the Honor to accept it Madam, not as a fine
likeness, or in itself a valuable work, but, as an acknowledgement
of the grateful Respect with which I have the Honor to be

                        Madam
                        Your very much obliged
                            and Humble Servant
                                Jn Trumbull

Mrs Washington

John Trumbull *to* Martha Washington

London, England · October 7, 1796

THERE WAS NO JOB DESCRIPTION, no statutory acknowledgment of her existence. When George Washington took the oath of office as President, his wife, Martha, sailed into uncharted waters as First Lady. ❧ Of course, she wasn't known as the First Lady. That title didn't enter the public vocabulary until several decades later—and in the meantime no one knew what to call her. ("Lady Washington" is what many people settled on, an indication of the dignity with which she comported herself.) No one knew exactly what she was supposed to do, either, so the redoubtable Mrs. Washington had to create a workable role for herself.

She didn't much like the job. Complaining that she felt "more like a state prisoner than anything else," she nonetheless was "determined to be cheerful and happy, in whatever situation I may be." Although she had a lively mind and doubtless served as her husband's confidante on many occasions, she took no active part in politics, preferring instead to do what she had been doing for years—maintaining a stable household for her husband and presiding graciously over the social functions that his position required. She played the role well: Abigail Adams described her as "one of those unassuming characters who create Love and Esteem."

In this letter, famed artist John Trumbull tells the First Lady that he is sending her, "as an acknowledgement of . . . grateful respect," an engraving of one of his portraits of her husband. Apparently she liked it, as it is still at their home, Mount Vernon. The letter gives us no insight into her mind or personality, which apparently is just what she would have wanted. Soon after George Washington died in 1799, his widow burned their private correspondence. ❧

John Trumbull presented this engraving of his 1796 portrait as a gift to Martha Washington.

Philadelphia Xbre the 17th 1796

Madam.

When public charity is requested, J think no one is more
obliged to contribute but those who are making their
fortune by the Public.
This induced me to have my Elephant exhibited for the
benefit of the sufferers by the late fire at Savanah —
to succeed in my End, it is necessary to have some
patrons; J could not look upon any one more qualified
than you, Madam, known as you are every where
by those qualities of humanity which makes the
only difference amongst Mankind.
You will, J make no doubt excuse the liberty

A. St. Mary *to* Martha Washington

Philadelphia, Pennsylvania • December 17, 1796

THE WASHINGTONS HAD BARELY SETTLED INTO their new roles when people started making requests of the President's wife. Many of the writers begged the First Lady for some memento of the much revered President (she reportedly got so many requests for a lock of her husband's hair that she started sending hanks of horsehair in response), while others wanted her to use her influence to further a cause or advance a career. ❧ Like many others, this letter asks Mrs. Washington for something, but it's not a run-of-the-mill request. It's all about a disastrous conflagration and a wondrous pachyderm, both of which were of considerable interest to Americans of the day but don't figure prominently in modern-day histories of the fledgling Republic.

On November 26, 1796, in Savannah, Georgia, a fire broke out in a bakeshop and quickly spread in every direction. It was neither the first nor the last major blaze to sweep through the place, but it was one of the worst. By the time it was extinguished, well over 200 buildings—almost two-thirds of the city, by some accounts—lay in ruins. Property losses were estimated at more than a million dollars, scores of businesses were destroyed, and hundreds of families were left homeless and destitute.

Touched by reports of the suffering of their fellow citizens in Georgia, many Americans organized relief efforts, passing the collection plate at hastily convened public meetings and organizing bake sales and charity bazaars. Among those who wanted to do his part was Mr. A. St. Mary of Philadelphia, who wrote this letter to Martha Washington, asking her to lend her name as patroness of a benefit exhibition of his elephant.

Somewhat surprisingly, elephants have a fairly long history in America. The first one was brought here by a sea captain named Jacob Crowninshield, who purchased a two-year-old calf in India for $450, loaded it onto his ship—not an easy thing to do, surely—and delivered it to New York in 1796. The animal immediately went on exhibition and proved such a success that it was promptly purchased by a shrewd businessman for a sum that amply repaid Captain Crowninshield for his trouble. For the next several years, this pioneering pachyderm, which apparently was never given a name, traveled up and down the East Coast, drawing awestruck crowds wherever it went. By the time of the California gold rush, the phrase "going to see the elephant" had entered the language as a popular euphemism for embarking on an adventure.

In 1861, King Mongkut of Siam was so distressed to learn that America was woefully undersupplied with elephants that he generously offered to send President Abraham Lincoln a few pairs of the useful animals so they could be "turned loose in forests" and allowed to "increase till there be large herds." Lincoln turned down the gift, but that didn't stop individual entrepreneurs from introducing an occasional elephant to our shores. In the 1880s, famed showman P. T. Barnum purchased one named Jumbo from the London Zoo (despite the anguished pleas of thousands of English schoolchildren), turned the 11-foot-tall animal into a publicity phenomenon, and made his very name a synonym for "huge."

Around the turn of the century, audiences thrilled to the pugilistic exploits of a boxing elephant named, appropriately enough, John L. Sullivan. More recently, art critics and buyers have heaped praise on the canvases produced by elephant artists in zoos from Anchorage to Buffalo to Phoenix. Still, relations between elephants and Americans haven't always been cordial. In Unicoi County, Tennessee, an elephant named Mary was arrested and hanged—a truly challenging task, involving a huge derrick and lengths of logging chain—after attacking and killing one of her handlers in 1916.

Of course, this long and eventful saga of spectacle and tragedy, cruelty and silliness, had not yet been written when A. St. Mary sent his letter to Martha Washington. Laying on the flattery in an effort to secure the First Lady's patronage, he silkily insists that he wouldn't dream of bothering her if she weren't "known . . . every where by those qualities of humanity which makes the only difference amongst Mankind." He even sweetens the pot by offering her some tickets "for the persons of your circle of acquaintance."

It is unknown whether St. Mary's blandishments persuaded Mrs. Washington to agree to be the patroness of the elephant exhibition, or whether she made use of her free tickets, though she is known to have attended the circus on a couple of occasions. If she didn't visit the exhibition, whether as patroness or mere spectator, the First Lady missed a remarkable spectacle, judging by an eye-catching broadside printed in Boston in 1797. The elephant so engagingly pictured must be the one that Crowninshield brought from India, since it is said to be four years old, which is about how old the enterprising captain's import would have been at the time. It must also be the same elephant referred to in St. Mary's letter, since it is described as having just arrived from an appearance in Philadelphia, and it's hard to imagine that there was more than one of these creatures making the rounds of eastern cities in 1797.

The text assures readers that the elephant is not only "most curious and surprising" but also highly intelligent and altogether worthy of its reputation as "the most respectable Animal in the world." However, in a hint that this paragon has a darker side to its nature, the broadside urges visitors to leave their important papers at home, since the elephant has been known to destroy them. This annoying proclivity is hardly surprising, since we are told that the animal has a serious drinking problem. As if that weren't bad enough, the poor beast is no doubt embarrassed by the fact that at least one observer—a minister, no less—stoutly insisted that "he" was unmistakably female.

It's enough to make any elephant cranky—and it explains the devilish gleam in his (or is it "her"?) eye. ❧

The arrival of the first elephant in the United States prompted this broadside by D. Bowen in 1797.

THE
Elephant,

ACCORDING to the account of the celebrated BUFFON, is the most respectable Animal in the world. In size he surpasses all other terrestrial creatures; and by his intelligence, he makes as near an approach to man, as matter can approach spirit. A sufficient proof that there is not too much said of the knowledge of this animal is, that the Proprietor having been absent for ten weeks, the moment he arrived at the door of his apartment, and spoke to the keeper, the animal's knowledge was beyond any doubt confirmed by the cries he uttered forth, till his Friend came within reach of his trunk, with which he caressed him, to the astonishment of all those who saw him. This most curious and surprising animal is just arrived in this town, from Philadelphia, where he will stay but a few weeks.——————————— He is only four years old, and weighs about 3000 weight, but will not have come to his full growth till he shall be between 30 and 40 years old. He measures from the end of his trunk to the tip of his tail 15 feet 8 inches, round the body 10 feet 6 inches, round his head 7 feet 2 inches, round his leg, above the knee, 3 feet 3 inches, round his ankle 2 feet 2 inches. He eats 130 weight a day, and drinks all kinds of spirituous liquors; some days he has drank 30 bottles of porter, drawing the corks with his trunk. He is so tame that he travels loose, and has never attempted to hurt any one. He appeared on the stage, at the New Theatre in Philadelphia, to the great satisfaction of a respectable audience.

A respectable and convenient place is fitted up at Mr. VALENTINE's, head of the Market, for the reception of those ladies and gentlemen who may be pleased to view the greatest natural curiosity ever presented to the curious, and is to be seen from sun-rise, 'till sun-down, every Day in the Week, Sundays excepted.

☞ The Elephant having destroyed many papers of consequence, it is recommended to visitors not to come near him with such papers.

☞ Admittance, ONE QUARTER OF A DOLLAR.——Children, NINE PENCE.

Boston, August 18th, 1797.

BOSTON: Printed by D. BOWEN, at the COLUMBIAN MUSEUM Press, head of the Mall.

Presidents house Washington City, Nov. 2. 1800

My dearest friend

We arrived here last night, or rather yesterday at
one O Clock and here we dined and Slept. The Building is
in a State to be habitable. And now we wish for your
Company. The Account you give of the melancholly State
of our dear Brother Mr Cranch and his family is really
distressing and must Severely afflict you. I most cordially
Sympathize with you and them.

I have Seen only Mr Marshall and Mr Stoddert
General Wilkinson and the two Commissioners Mr Scott and
Mr Thornton.

I shall Say nothing of public affairs. I am
very glad you consented to come on, for you would have been
more anxious at Quincy than here, and I, to all my other
Solicitudines Mordaces as Horace calls them i.e. "biting
Cares" Should have added a great deal on your Account.
Besides it is fit and proper that you and I Should retire
together and not one before the other

John Adams *to* Abigail Adams

Washington, D.C. • November 2, 1800

MORE THAN A THOUSAND LETTERS FROM JOHN ADAMS to his wife, Abigail, have survived, and almost every one of them offers proof that their enduring relationship was founded not only on deep affection but also on mutual respect. Although she had no formal education, Abigail was one of the most widely read women of her day. What's more, she wasn't shy about expressing her opinion, and John relied on her candor. He wasn't exaggerating when he wrote her in 1797, "I must now repeat this with zeal and earnestness. I can do nothing without you." ❧ During his

lengthy career in politics and public service, Adams held many positions—from delegate to the Continental Congress to American minister to France—that kept him away from Abigail for months at a time. The couple bridged the miles between them with a stream of correspondence in which Abigail shared her views on everything from the dangers of too-frequent popular elections ("No engine can be more fatally employed . . . to corrupt and destroy the morals of the people") to low-cut dresses that make women "literally look like nursing mothers."

They separated again when President Adams moved the government to the new federal capital on the Potomac. His official residence, like most of the city, was still unfinished: The grounds were an expanse of weeds and mud and workmen's shacks; the only entrance to the house was through the basement; a narrow, winding service stair provided the only access to the upper floors; and the rooms—many of which had not even been plastered—were littered with wood shavings and a scattering of shabby furniture. The only hint of grandeur was provided by Gilbert Stuart's full-length

portrait of Washington, which was to play a memorable role in White House history a few years later.

Abigail had been uneasy about her husband's living in the building, telling her niece, "I fear it would prove his death to go into a House so green as I think the Presidents House must and will be," but Adams insisted on moving in on November 1, 1800. The next morning he sent this letter to the woman who was much on his mind, as always, as he wandered through the echoing rooms. "The Building is in a State to be habitable," he writes. "And now we wish for your Company." He closes with a prayer that has achieved lasting—and well-deserved—fame: "I pray Heaven to bestow the best of Blessings on this House and all that shall hereafter inhabit it. May none but honest and wise Men ever rule under this roof."

Abigail soon joined her husband in the President's House, where she hung laundry in the unfinished East Room. More than a century later, President Franklin Roosevelt had Adams's benediction carved on the mantel in the State Dining Room. ❧

Dear Madam   Washington June 13. 04.

The affectionate sentiments which you have had the goodness to express in your letter of May 20. towards my dear departed daughter, have awakened in me sensibilities natural to the occasion, & recalled your kindnesses to her which I shall ever remember with gratitude & friendship. I can assure you with truth they had made an indelible impression on her mind, and that, to the last, on our meetings after long separations, whether I had heard lately of you, and how you did, were among the earliest of her enquiries. in giving you this assurance I perform a sacred duty for her, & at the same time am thankful for the occasion furnished me of expressing my regret that circumstances should have arisen which have seemed to draw a line of separation between us. the friendship with which you honoured me has ever been valued, and fully reciprocated, & altho' events have been passing which might be trying to some minds, I never believed yours to be of that kind, nor felt that my own was. neither my estimate of your character, nor the esteem founded in that, have ever been lessened for a single moment although doubts whether it would be acceptable may have forbidden manifestations of it.   Mr. Adams's friendships & mine began at an earlier date. it accompanied us thro' long & important scenes. the different conclusions we had drawn from our political reading & reflections were not permitted to lessen mutual esteem, each party being conscious they were the result of an honest conviction in the other. like differences of opinion existing among our fellow citizens attached them to the one or the other of us, and produced a rivalship in their minds which did not exist in ours. we never stood in one another's way, for if either had been withdrawn at any time, his favorers would not have gone over to the other, but would have sought for some one of homogeneous opinions. this consideration was sufficient to keep down all jealousy between us, & to guard our friendship

24446   Mrs. Adams

THOMAS JEFFERSON *to* ABIGAIL ADAMS

Washington, D.C. • June 13, 1804

THE CLOSEST FRIENDS MAKE THE BITTEREST ENEMIES, and if breaking up is hard to do, making up is sometimes even harder. ❧ John Adams and Thomas Jefferson embodied all that was best and brightest in the remarkable generation of thinker-patriots who shepherded America through its transformation from colony to republic. Articulate and tenacious in their devotion to the cause of independence, they envisioned a new kind of democracy, crafted the rhetoric to inspire their compatriots, and took bold steps to turn their vision into reality. What's more, despite differences in their

political philosophies and party affiliations, they were devoted friends, bound not only by a shared delight in intellectual pursuits but also by ties that sprang from the heart.

Then, at the very beginning of the 19th century, it all fell apart. Just before leaving the Presidency, Adams made some appointments that Jefferson thought undermined his authority. For his part, Adams believed that Jefferson had betrayed him by aligning himself with some who were Adams's enemies. Both men were right, both were wrong—but the wounds were so deep that they stopped speaking to each other.

That's where matters stood in 1804, when Jefferson's daughter, Maria Eppes, died in childbirth. As a girl, Maria had lived for a while with John and Abigail Adams in London, so when Abigail learned of her death, she sent a warm message of condolence to Jefferson. This letter is his reply.

After thanking her for her thoughtfulness in his hour of grief, he assures her of his continued high regard for her: "Neither my estimate of your character, nor the esteem founded in that, have ever been lessened for a single moment. . . ." Then, in a somewhat startling shift of focus, he launches into an explanation for his rift with Abigail's husband, studding the passage with evidence of his continued affection for his estranged friend. "I maintain for him, and shall carry into private life," he writes, "an uniform and high measure of respect and good will."

Abigail correctly interpreted Jefferson's words as a hesitant but sincere invitation to reconciliation, and she acted on it in subsequent correspondence with him. It took time to bring the two men together, but when Jefferson learned that Adams had said to a mutual friend, "I always loved Jefferson and still love him," the last barriers fell. Before long the two men were writing directly to each other, reminiscing about the old days and expressing great pleasure in having rekindled their friendship at last, with Abigail's help.

The two old lions remained close for the rest of their lives. When Adams died in 1826, his last words were, "Jefferson still lives." He was wrong: Jefferson had breathed his last just a few hours earlier—dying, like Adams, on America's 50th birthday. ❧

Extract from a letter written to my
Sister unpublished in the "sketch of my Life" written
for the "National Portrait Gallery."

Tuesday Augt. 23d 1814.

Dear Sister. My husband left me yesterday
morn.g to join Gen. Winder. — He enquired
anxiously whether I had courage, or firmness
to remain in the President's house until
his return, on the morrow, or succeeding day
and on my assurance that I had no fear
but for him and the success of our army, he left me,
beseeching me to take care of myself, and of
the cabinet papers, public and private. —
I have since rec.d two despatches from him,
written with a pencil; the last is alarming,
because he desires I should be ready at a
moment's warning to enter my carriage and
leave the city; that the enemy seemed stronger
than had been reported, and that it might
happen that they would reach the city,
with intention to destroy it. × × ×
× × × I am accordingly ready; I
have pressed as many cabinet papers into
trunks as to fill one carriage; our private
property must be sacrificed, as it is impossible

49948

DOLLEY MADISON *to* ANNA CUTTS

Washington, D.C. · *August 23, 1814*

IN THIS LETTER TO HER SISTER, First Lady Dolley Madison conveys a breathless sense of immediacy in her account of one of the most shameful episodes in American history. ❧ The War of 1812 had just entered its third year when British admiral Thomas Cochrane decided to humiliate the upstart Americans by destroying their capital. Scattering defenders and sending residents into panicked flight, the British marched into Washington, torched the Capitol, the President's House, and several other buildings, then returned to their ships. ❧ Dolley's original letter has

been lost; what we see here is a copy that she made many years later. She writes on August 23 that she has loaded a carriage with important documents and is "ready at a moment's warning to . . . leave the city." Then, on the 24th: "Two messengers covered with dust, come to bid me fly. . . ." In a courageous and justly celebrated act that puts her escort "in a very bad humor," she insists on rescuing a portrait of Washington—and then she is gone, telling her sister, ". . . where I shall be tomorrow, I cannot tell!"

A few days later, the President and First Lady returned to the devastated capital city, where they occupied rented quarters for the remainder of Madison's term. In 1817, President James Monroe moved into the rebuilt White House. The portrait that Dolley saved hangs in the East Room. ❧

William Strickland engraved this northeast view of the White House after it was damaged by fire in 1814.

Newton Upper Falls, Mass.
Jan 7, 1853.

Mr & Mrs Peirce,

    Dear friends,

        We have read to day of the loss of your dear Son at Andover with the most painful feelings. We deeply sympathise with you in the desolation which has so suddenly and unexpectedly blasted the beautiful prospects of the future. The spirit of the dear one is now in a world of light however desolate the hearts of his parents and we can only point to Him who is able & willing to sooth & heal their He has broken and wounded. We wish we could be with you & by our presence a little even of the grief which has overwhelmed you could be mitigated.

        We remain with the warmest affection

        Your friends

        A. H. Dearborn

        H. N. Dearborn

A. D. and N. D. Dearborn *to* Jane Pierce

Newton Upper Falls, Massachusetts • January 4, 1853

Jane Pierce *to* Benny Pierce

Washington, D.C. • January 1853

No First Lady entered the White House under a greater burden of grief than did Jane Pierce in 1853. A painfully shy woman who grew up in a conservative and deeply religious home, Jane despised politics. She was understandably dismayed when the young man who was courting her, Franklin Pierce, was elected to the New Hampshire Legislature and then to the U.S. House of Representatives, but she married him anyway, perhaps thinking she could persuade him to abandon the political arena. Instead, he won a seat in the U.S. Senate. ✻

Jane's life soon descended into tragedy. Her first two children died when very young. The third child, a boy named Benjamin, became the focus of Jane's affections, but even his lively presence couldn't relieve her frequent spells of depression. Alarmed by his wife's increasingly fragile health, Pierce resigned from the Senate and returned to New Hampshire. He turned down the post of attorney general that President James Polk offered him and served honorably in the Mexican War, and then a hopelessly deadlocked Democratic Convention chose him as its compromise candidate for President. Pierce felt that he had no choice but to accept the nomination of his party, and he won the 1852 election in a landslide. Feeling utterly betrayed by her husband and dismayed by the prospect of life in Washington, Jane fainted when she heard the news.

Then came the final, crushing blow. A few days before they were to journey to Washington for the Inauguration, the Pierces were passengers in a railroad car that jumped the track and tumbled down an embankment. The President-elect and his wife were unhurt, but 11-year-old Benny was killed before their eyes. Prostrated by grief, Jane was unable to accompany her husband to Washington. She eventually joined him and tried to play the demanding role of hostess, confessing to her sister that she found it "much less trying to meet perfect strangers than those who are in any way associated with the past." Still, public appearances remained painful for her and everyone around her, and people started calling her "the shadow in the White House."

It was during this period of most profound grief that President and Mrs. Pierce received this letter from some friends in Massachusetts. Employing the extravagantly sentimental language that Victorian-era writers considered appropriate to the occasion, the Dearborns offer their sympathy "in the desolation which has so suddenly and unexpectedly blasted the beautiful prospects of the future" and pointlessly remind the Pierces that "the spirit of the dear one is now in a wild flight"—a fact from which the heartbroken mother probably did not draw much comfort.

Unwilling to let her "dear one" go, the stricken First Lady reportedly consulted a famous pair of mediums in an attempt to communicate with Benny. She also wrote long letters to the dead child, and one of them is shown here, a rambling discourse that sprawls over the closely written pages in a wild, unbridled outburst of agony that cannot find release. It is hard to read, not only because the handwriting is cramped and faded but also because the emotions it bares are so deep and raw.

Every aspect of grief is here. Jane castigates herself for having been an imperfect parent (". . . my dear son, how much I feel my own faults in regard to you—I know that I did not take the right way and should have dealt with you very gently often when I judged hastily and spoke harshly. I can see that I was 'unreasonable' and sometimes almost wonder that you loved me at all"). She tries to find consolation in religion (". . . oh to think of you kneeling by me at our evening prayer tonight, dear child—has not the Savior made you His as we so often asked. But now I must kneel alone and beg for strength and support under this crushing sorrow, that the Blessed Savior would comfort the heart of your pain stricken Mother . . ."). Perhaps most heart-wrenching of all, she expresses the sense of incompleteness felt by anyone who experiences the death of a loved one: "I do not know how to go on without you—you were my comfort dear—far more than you thought. . . . Oh! you were indeed 'a part of mine and of your father's heart.' When I have told you dear boy how much you depended on me, and felt that you could not do without me—I did not say too how much I depended on you."

Finally, she closes with a fantasy in which everything is as it used to be: ". . . and now this Sabbath evening you will come in fancy before me and I sit close by you, with your hand in mine perhaps, or you will lean against me on the sofa, or . . . sit on my lap a little while and we talk together and say hymns and then play and then by and by you go to bed first putting your arms around me and laying your dear head on my shoulder and then you get in your bed and we have our Sabbath night kiss."

Reading this, we understand why Jane, sitting alone in a White House draped in black, wrote to her sister, "I long to fly away sometimes, I hardly know where, only to freedom & quiet."

Later in her husband's Presidency, Jane's spirits improved somewhat. She occasionally went shopping with her friend Varina Davis, the future first lady of the Confederacy, and attended congressional debates over the expansion of slavery, but her health remained poor. By the time she moved out of the White House, she was severely weakened by tuberculosis. Seeking a salubrious climate, the Pierces traveled to the Caribbean and Europe before returning to New England for good. Jane carried Benny's Bible with her for much of the rest of her life, and when she died in 1863 she was buried near him. ❧

#96-2

My precious child — I must write to you, altho' you are never to see it, a kind — How I long to see you and say something to you as if you were as you always have been — until these last three dreadful weeks, near me — oh! how precious do those days now seem. my darling boy — and how should I have prized the days passed with you had I suspected they might be so short — dear dear child — I cannot bear to think of that agonizing time, when I had just seen you all alive to what was passing around and near me, but not near enough — oh had you but been been within reach of your dear father's a moment changed my dear boy's breath from into a lifeless one — inscrutable to your parents' agony — But your spirit yourself, my dear one — was not your Redeeming Saviour ready to receive you? your sweet little mother, dear Aunt Lauren, but you are beyond my knowledge at once — oh, I trust in joy — but I would fain have kept you here — I know not how to go on without you — you were my constant delight for more than you thought. I was thinking how pleasantly we should go on together when we found ourselves at home again — and I would do every thing to make you love me and have confidence in me, and bring you along gently and sweetly — oh! you were indeed, a part of mine and of your father's heart — When I have told you dear boy how much you depended on me, and felt that you could not do without me" I did not say too, how much I depended on you — and oh! my precious boy how gladly would I recall all that was unreasonable or hasty — a **mistakes in my conduct** toward you — I see surely, and I did frequently see afterward that I had wronged you — and would gladly have acknowledged it only that I feared it might weaken your confidence in me and perhaps on that account not be as well for you — and now I am here again dear boy — oh what anguish was mine on returning without you, and feeling that it must still be so, while there — to see you little bed that you loved so much — and which I look at so many times in the day, and at night feel as if I must see it made out again and the clothes turned down for you — and unconsciously look in the morning for you — and listen for you — bright cheerful voices your little "good morrow" — and oh! to look around and see your books and everything so connected with you own dear self — and now on the little

Wingamatube. Asking
for something to be done
St Louis Mo Feby 1858
to prevent whiskey being
sold among his red
brethren.

Lady wilt thou permit the dark browed Son of the
of a Chippeway to address his petition to thee: he is told thou canst speak
in the ears of thine uncle the President, and that he will give heed to what
thou suggest; Years ago i left my Forest home to be educated among
the good white People, last Summer when the leaves were green
and the flowers were in bloom i thought i would go and visit my
People; After journeying many days. My heart was again gladdened
with the sight of the woody Grove and Silvery Waters. where the
wigwams of my fathers had once Stood. but now alas; all
was Silent and and desolate. only the numerous Graves that
dotted the hillsides told the fate of my once numerous kindred.
the Whiskey Demon; had been there, and with his poisonous breath
he had Slain my people. as a destroying angel he had made desolate
the once quiet and happy homes of the Simple Children of nature
too well i understood the cause; for when the wise men of our
Nations were Gathered in council; they declared that our
Great Father, the President and his sages. had enacted wise and
just laws in our behalf; but that the Men that had

& yours
Wingamatube,

WINGEMATUB *to* HARRIET LANE

Address Unknown • February 4, 1858

WHEN LIFELONG BACHELOR JAMES BUCHANAN became President, he asked his niece Harriet Lane to serve as his official hostess. It was an inspired choice, since Miss Lane proved to be one of the most gracious, accomplished, and popular women who ever occupied the White House. ❧ Harriet was no stranger to the intricacies of protocol, having accompanied her uncle to London when he was named Ambassador to the Court of St. James's in 1854. Queen Victoria was deeply impressed by the young woman's intelligence, beauty, and poise,

and these same qualities endeared her to Americans (and won her a number of suitors, whom she dismissed as "pleasant but dreadfully troublesome") when she returned to Washington and moved into the Executive Mansion.

Possessing a lively mind that would not allow her to limit her activities to making charming conversation and working out seating arrangements for dinner parties, Harriet became interested in improving conditions on the nation's Indian reservations. Her tireless advocacy on their behalf inspired many Native Americans to call her their "great mother" and led one member of the Chippewa tribe to write this letter.

In stilted but compelling language that he doubtless learned from Christian missionaries, a "dark browned Son of the Chippeway" named Wingematub describes the evils being visited on his people by the current federal agent, a "Great Drunkard" who ensures that "whiskey is as plentiful as water." Having heard that Harriet's uncle "will give heed to what thou sayest,"

Wingematub implores her to ask the President to remove the agent and the "Locusts of Egypt" who are his cohorts before "the dark wines of oblivion cover us."

To her credit, Harriet looked into the matter and took steps to improve educational opportunities and medical care among the Chippewa. As a result, "Harriet Lane" became a popular name for Native American children. ❧

Harriet Lane, niece of President James Buchanan, was widely admired for her beauty and generosity.

Rochester May 7th 1861

Mrs Lincoln,

Dear Lady please excuse the
freedom I take of addressing a few lines to you
I am an American Girl, my parents were
born in the State of Vermont, but I was
born in the City of Troy N.Y. I have been
employed for a few years back writing the
Mail, for the Independence, at the Independent
office Number 5 Beekman St New York City
while in this City I become acquainted with
a German whom I married May 10 1860
only one Year ago, He belongs to that Class
of Sober honest industrious Germans who
are so anxiously striving to beautify and
in rich our beloved Country, he is a great
admirer of Mr Lincoln, and is ready to give
up his life for the defence of his adopted Country

Helen M. Rauschnabel *to* Mary Todd Lincoln

Rochester, New York • May 7, 1861

LIKE A GOOD MANY PEOPLE OF HER DAY, First Lady Mary Todd Lincoln was a firm believer in the power of omens and the presence of otherworldly spirits in the mortal realm. ❧ On more than one occasion after the death of her son Willie she employed mediums and held séances in the White House in an effort to contact the dead child, with Cabinet members and President Lincoln himself sometimes in attendance. A newspaper account in 1863 described what happened at one of these sessions: Invisible spirits pinched the ears of the Secretary of War and pulled the beard of the Secretary of the Navy, a pair of candelabras rose nearly to the ceiling, chairs and tables moved about the room, lamps flared and dimmed, cryptic messages appeared on sheets of writing paper, and various loud rappings were heard. Obviously viewing the goings-on as a lark, the President cracked jokes throughout the séance—and no wonder, since the whole event had a definite Abbott and Costello air about it. His wife, we can assume, was not amused.

Given her fascination with spiritualism and the importance of dreams and signs, Mary Lincoln must have been very interested in this letter from a young woman in Rochester, New York, who writes to tell the First Lady about a dream. It began, she says, with a storm, and then President Lincoln appeared with his head "reard above the lightnings flash and thunder bolt." Standing "in the western part of the firmament . . . crowned with honors & coverd with Laurels," Lincoln "looked very smiling," and the scene was so glorious that the dreamer burst into song: "A voice from the North has proclaimed the glad Morn / And Slavery is ended & Freedom is born. . . ." Mrs. Rauschnabel tells Mrs. Lincoln that she hopes this strange blend of melodrama and oratorio "might be a comfort to you in these perilous times," and, knowing the First Lady's bent, it probably was.

A few days before his assassination, the President had a strange dream of his own. He later told friends that in the dream, he wandered through the White House, seeing no one, but hearing the sobs of people "grieving as if their hearts would break." Entering the East Room, he found soldiers standing guard over a corpse whose face was shrouded from view. When he asked who had died, the answer was, "The President. He was killed by an assassin."

Although he shrugged the morbid dream off as a meaningless nightmare, Lincoln admitted to having been "strangely annoyed" by it. When he related his strange vision to Mary, the shaken woman reportedly scolded him for having told her and flounced out of the room. No doubt Helen Rauschnabel's dream was more to the superstitious First Lady's liking. ❧

My Dear Husband.

I wrote you on
yesterday, yet omitted
a very important item with -
Elizabeth Keckley, who is me
and is working for the Contra-
-band Association, at Wash-
is authorised by the White
part of the concern by a
written document - to coll
-ect any thing for them -
here that, she can - She has
been very unsuccessful - She
says the immense number
of Contrabands in W - are
suffering intensely, many
without bed covering & having
to use any bits of carpeting
will bring you on the bill

42387

MARY TODD LINCOLN *to* ABRAHAM LINCOLN

New York, New York • November 3, 1862

THIS LETTER FROM MARY LINCOLN TO HER HUSBAND, written while the First Lady was visiting New York in the fall of 1862, introduces us to a remarkable woman named Elizabeth Keckley. Born a slave in Virginia, Keckley became a skilled seamstress and eventually accumulated enough money to buy her freedom. Soon after settling in Washington, she became Mrs. Lincoln's dressmaker—and her trusted friend and confidante as well. ❧ Keckley was touched by the plight of the fugitive slaves commonly known as contrabands, who flocked to Washington in search of a better

life. "Poor dusky children of slavery," she later wrote of them, ". . . you were not prepared for the new life that opened before you, and the great masses of the North . . . learned to speak of you as an idle,

dependent race." With the help of friends, she founded the Contraband Relief Association to help those who had discovered that "independence brought with it the cares and vexations of poverty."

When Keckley told her employer about the work of the society, the First Lady immediately promised to contribute $200 for the purchase of blankets and clothing. In this letter she tells the President what she has done. Her smooth words—"this sum, I am sure, you will not object to being used in this way"—are probably unnecessary: The President is already aware of his wife's free-spending habits and doubtless realizes that argument would be fruitless.

Because she was Kentucky-born and had relatives who fought for the Confederacy, Mary Lincoln was sometimes accused of harboring southern sympathies. This letter, demonstrating her compassion for those whose labor had long fueled the southern economy and whose emancipation her husband would soon proclaim, refutes that charge. The President's wife was no traitor. ❧

Elizabeth Keckley's **Behind the Scenes** *provided a glimpse of life in the White House in the early 1860s.*

Executive Mansion,

Washington, August 8, 1863.

My dear Wife:

All as well as usual, and no particular trouble any way. I put the money into the Treasury at five per cent, with the privilege of withdrawing it any time upon thirty day's notice. I suppose you are glad to learn this. Tell dear Tad, poor "Nanny Goat," is lost; and Mrs. Cuthbert & I are in distress about it.

The day you left Nanny was found resting herself, and chewing her little cud, on the middle of Tad's bed. But now she's gone! The gardener kept complaining that she destroyed the flowers, till it was concluded to bring her down to the White House. This was done, and the second day she had disappeared, and has not been heard of since. This is the last we know of poor "Nanny"

The weather continues dry, and excessively warm here.

Nothing very important occurring. The election in Kentucky has gone very strongly right. Old Mr. Wickliffe got ugly, as you know, ran for Governor, and is terribly beaten. Upon Mr. Crittenden's death, Brutus Clay, Cassius' brother, was put on the track for Congress, and is largely elected. Mr. Menzies, who, as we thought, behaved

25144

Abraham Lincoln *to* Mary Todd Lincoln

Washington, D.C. • *August 8, 1863 & April 28, 1864*

MANY PEOPLE BELIEVE THAT A HOUSE IS NOT A HOME unless it has animals in it. If that's true, the White House has been a homey place for much of its history. ❧ John Quincy Adams kept an alligator for a while (he probably felt obliged to, since it was a gift from the Marquis de Lafayette), and a kid in Texas once mailed a horned toad to President Eisenhower. Jefferson had a pet mockingbird, while Andrew Johnson reportedly made do with a couple of white mice he found in his bedroom. To reduce groundskeeping costs, the Tafts turned a cow named Pauline Wayne loose on the White House lawn. The Coolidges were avid animal lovers whose pets included a raccoon that was walked on a leash and liked to drape itself around the President's neck. Caroline Kennedy had a pony named Macaroni, and there was a pony named Algonquin in the menagerie of Theodore Roosevelt's family—along with, among other things, a bear, a badger, various snakes, a blue macaw, several guinea pigs, and a one-legged rooster.

Not surprisingly, lots of dogs have made their home in the Executive Mansion. In the 1920s President Harding's Airedale had a chair of its own at Cabinet meetings, and in the 1960s LBJ caused an uproar by lifting his beagles, Him and Her, by the ears and insisting that they liked it. Other White House dogs have included King Tut and Pat, the Hoovers' German shepherds; Vicky and King Timahoe, the Nixons' poodle and Irish setter, respectively; and Millie and Spot, the mother-and-daughter pets of the father-and-son Bushes.

The Lincolns had goats.

Tad Lincoln had a pony, though he seemed to lose interest in it after his brother Willie died, and he later made a pet of a lucky turkey named Jack after rescuing the bird from a rendezvous with the White House oven. After the boy saw some goats one day and expressed interest in them, the President bought a pair and named them Nanny and Nanko. They had the run of the White House, thoroughly—and repeatedly—wrecking the flower beds and even sleeping with Tad once in a while. On one memorable occasion, Tad hitched them to a chair and raced like a charioteer through the East Room, shouting "Get out of the way there!" and sending a group of visiting Bostonians scurrying for cover. The President managed to stifle his laughter; the First Lady didn't laugh at all.

In her 1868 memoir, seamstress Elizabeth Keckley wrote that the goats knew the sound of Lincoln's voice and "would come bounding to his side" when he called them. She recalled an afternoon when he was watching the goats from a window: "Just then both goats looked up at the window and shook their heads as if they would say, 'How d'ye do, old friend?' 'See, Madam Elizabeth,' exclaimed the President in a tone of enthusiasm, 'my pets recognize me. How earnestly they look! They go again; what jolly fun!'" While it's highly unlikely that Lincoln ever uttered these stilted phrases, the story suggests that he enjoyed the goats as much as his son did.

When Tad was away from Washington he liked to be kept informed of his pets' activities, so reports on their carryings-on figured prominently in the President's letters to his absent wife and son. In the letter shown here, written in August 1863 while the First Lady and Tad were on a visit to the White Mountains in New Hampshire, he has some bad news: "Tell dear Tad, poor 'Nanny Goat' is lost; and Mrs. Cuthbert [a member of the White House staff] & I are in distress about it."

The President was staying, as the family always did during the hot summer months, at the Soldiers' Home on the northern outskirts of Washington. Nanny was causing such a ruckus—not only destroying the flower beds, as usual, but also "resting herself, and chewing her little cud, on the middle of Tad's bed"—that it was finally decided to send her into exile at the White House. "This was done," Lincoln writes, "and the second day she had disappeared, and has not been heard of since—This is the last we know of poor 'Nanny.'" We have to wonder whether the much aggrieved gardener and housekeeper colluded in Nanny's "disappearance," but if so, their efforts were in vain. The goat eventually turned up, giving no indication that the trauma had persuaded her to mend her ways.

The second piece of correspondence that is shown here, a brief telegram written in April 1864 while Mrs. Lincoln and Tad were in New York, is much less dramatic but even more engaging. In a message of just a few lines, the President indicates that he recognizes his place in the White House hierarchy. "Tell Tad the goats and father are very well," he writes, "especially the goats."

Tad did not get to enjoy happy times with his father and the goats much longer. Less than a year after this telegram was sent, Lincoln was assassinated at Ford's Theatre. Tad himself died in 1871, most likely of tuberculosis.

According to Elizabeth Keckley, Mary Lincoln was never fond of the goats. Unable to stand the sight of them after her husband's death, she gave the animals away. ✒

Anthony Berger photographed Lincoln and his son Tad in this tender scene on February 9, 1864.

Executive Mansion.

Washington, April 28. 1864.

Mrs. A. Lincoln
        Metropolitan Hotel
                New York.

                    The draft will go to
you— Tell Tad the goats and father are
very well— especially the goats.

                                A. Lincoln.

April 1864
Recd.
Sent
[?]

Page 48

April 29. 1865.

Dear Madam,

Though a stranger to you I cannot remain silent when so terrible a Calamity has fallen upon

stricken can look for comfort, in this hour of heavy affliction,

With the renewed Expression of true Sympathy, I remain, dear Madam, Your sincere

Z.99.29/72

QUEEN VICTORIA *to* MARY TODD LINCOLN

Isle of Wight, England · April 29, 1865

IN 1862, THE DEATH OF HER YOUNG SON WILLIE plunged First Lady Mary Todd Lincoln into such despair that her husband led her to a White House window, pointed to the distant insane asylum, and gently told her, "Try and control your grief or it will drive you mad, and we may have to send you there." Three years later, the assassination of President Lincoln sent her into new paroxysms of grief, and this time there was no husband to comfort her. Her friend Elizabeth Keckley reported that the White House echoed with "the wails of a broken heart, the wild unearthly shrieks, the wild tempestuous outbursts of grief from the soul."

Britain's Queen Victoria understood what Mary Lincoln was going through: The death of her own beloved husband, Albert, in 1861 had left her so shattered that some feared for her sanity. She was still shunning most public life when she sent this letter, heavily black-bordered in accordance with the custom of the day, to the First Lady.

Victoria writes not only as one public figure to another—but also, touchingly and intimately, as widow to widow. Acknowledging that she is still "utterly broken-hearted" by the loss of the man who was "the *Light* of my Life,—my Stay—*my All*," she says, in effect, the only thing that can be said in such a situation: I've been there, and I know how much it hurts. In a letter of reponse a few weeks later, the First Lady assured the widowed monarch that she was "deeply grateful" for the Queen's "expressions of tender sympathy, coming as they do from a heart which from its own Sorrow, can appreciate the intense grief, I now endure."

It took Mary Lincoln five weeks to feel strong enough to vacate the White House. For the next several years she continued to anguish over her husband's death. She wandered restlessly across Europe, spent herself into enormous debt, suffered the loss of her son Tad in 1871 (the third son she had to bury), and attempted suicide.

In desperation, her oldest son, Robert, had her declared insane and committed to a sanitarium—an act of betrayal for which she never fully forgave him. After four months of confinement, she was released to the custody of her sister. She died in 1882 and was laid to rest beside the martyred President.

Queen Victoria gradually emerged from her self-imposed seclusion in the late 1860s, although she continued to wear mourning for the rest of her long life. After she died in 1901, she was buried in the mausoleum that she had built for herself and Albert. A Latin inscription above the entrance reads, "Farewell best beloved, here at last I shall rest with thee, with thee in Christ I shall rise again."

It's a sentiment that Mary Lincoln would have approved—and understood. 🌼

To the wife of President Johnson.

Madam—

When I last wrote I said the President's friends
in Boston were increasing! And so it proved; for we
gave 5000 majority vote in Boston for John Quincy Adams
as Governor.   In the late trial I have been very anxious
that the President should be acquitted.

I prayed every night that a sufficient number
of honest men might be found in the senate
for his acquittal.   My prayers are answered.

The President, in the multiplicity of his cares,
will consider it proper in me to make this
request of you—viz:—that you advise him not
to attempt to change the nature of Stanton!
Not to change the nature of his enemies!
Tell him, Good Lady, patiently to allow the
tares to grow with the wheat.   Say to him, when
he is calm, after the hours of public business,
Give your enemies no opportunity henceforth
to injure you in any way. Tell him how
Socrates was abused by his enemies.

Yours Respectfully, Jonathan French
North-Hampton N: H. May 19th 1868.

20867

Jonathan French *to* Eliza Johnson

North Hampton, New Hampshire • May 19, 1868

Andrew Johnson's biography is the classic log-cabin-to-White-House story. As a struggling young tailor, Johnson was elected mayor of Greeneville, Tennessee, and moved swiftly up the political ladder, eventually serving in the U.S. Senate and as military governor of Tennessee before being tapped as Abraham Lincoln's running mate in 1864. Assassins led by John Wilkes Booth planned to kill Lincoln and Johnson on the horrific night of April 14, 1865, but Johnson escaped and was sworn in as President after Lincoln died. ✷ One of the

smartest things Johnson ever did was to marry Eliza McCardle in 1827. Johnson could barely read at the time, so Eliza

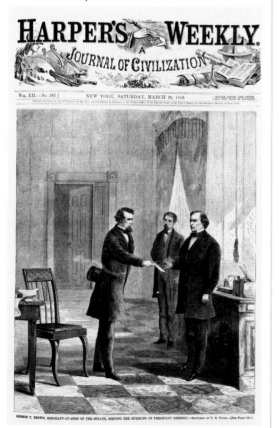

patiently helped him improve his writing and speaking skills and taught him arithmetic. Over the next several years, while her husband won elections, Eliza managed the family's finances and raised five children. By 1860, tuberculosis had made her a semi-invalid.

Life in the White House held little appeal for Eliza, who told a friend, "We are plain people from Tennessee, called here for a little time by a nation's calamity, and I hope too much will not be expected of us." She stayed mostly in her bedroom, crossing the hall to the President's office to calm him when his temper flared, which it did frequently.

In 1868, clashes with Congress led to Johnson's impeachment. Three days after he was acquitted by a margin of one vote, a supporter sent Eliza this letter, suggesting that she soothe her husband by reminding him "how Socrates was abused by his enemies." It was good advice, but Eliza didn't need it. Encouraging Andrew Johnson was something she'd been doing for years. ✷

Andrew Johnson is served an impeachment summons, as pictured on the March 28, 1868, cover of Harper's Weekly.

Dear Ulys
How many
years ago to day is that we
were Engaged?
Just such a day as this
too was it not?
Julia

Thirty-one years ago. I
was so frightened however that
I do not remember whither
it was warm or snowing.
Ulys.

Julia Grant *to* Ulysses S. Grant

Washington, D.C. • May 22, 1875

WE KNOW ULYSSES GRANT PRIMARILY AS A BRILLIANT military leader and thoroughly inept President—but judging by this note, he was also an extraordinarily loving husband who wasn't afraid of a tender phrase. ❧ Let's be honest here: Julia Grant was no beauty. She was plain and stout and cross-eyed, and none of it made a bit of difference to her husband. His adoration of her was so deep and unequivocal that when she considered surgery to correct her crossed eyes, he forbade it, saying he had fallen in love with her just as she was and didn't want her to change a thing. ❧

When they met, he was a young lieutenant with little to recommend him except for his friendship with Julia's brother, but the shy girl was smitten, and when her father objected that Grant was "too poor," she retorted that she was pretty poor herself and intended to marry him. She spent years as a traditional Army wife, tirelessly following her husband from post to post, standing by him when he briefly (and unsuccessfully) tried his hand at business, then packing up again when he rejoined the Army at the start of the Civil War. She rejoiced in the glory he won on the battlefield, and his triumph in the 1868 election marked the beginning of what she called "the happiest period" of her life: No one enjoyed being First Lady more than she did.

One day in 1875, while going through some old letters, Julia realized it was the anniversary of their engagement. She dashed off this brief note to "Ulys," who wrote two sentences in reply. The exchange is not at all flowery, but devotion and fond contentment shine through every word.

Their love never dimmed. Years after her husband's death in 1885, Julia wrote, "the light of his glorious fame still reaches out to me, falls upon me, and warms me." ❧

An unattributed and undated portrait of Ulysses and Julia Grant fails to capture their mutual devotion.

Baltimore March 8th 1881

Baltimore March 8 '81

Mrs Garfield

Hon & Respected Madam,
I come in behalf of suffering
humanity to beg that you
will attain to the high honor
of your predecessor, The Hon
Mrs Hayes where fame will
resound to the end of time
for her firmness to "Duty" in
opposition to custom, in
banishing the "Intoxicating
Cup" from The "White House".
Be firm, be strong, and God
will help you along; There
is no safety only in "Total
Abstinence", and its progress
must be onward for God is
so ordaining: and the time
will come when "Woman"
will exterminate him, the

75865

Mrs. E. C. Sloan *to* Lucretia Garfield

Baltimore, Maryland • March 8, 1881

BY ALL ACCOUNTS, LUCRETIA GARFIELD WAS A GENTLE, KINDLY WOMAN. But even the saintliest First Lady must find it annoying to constantly be urged to live up to the lofty standard set by her predecessor. ✒ It was all about temperance. The campaign to rid America of the evils of alcohol was a major social force in the late 19th century, culminating in the fearsome image of the hatchet-wielding Carry Nation storming through saloons like the wrath of God Himself. Long before the formidable Miss Nation appeared on the scene, however, one of the popular heroines of the temperance

movement was First Lady Lucy Hayes, wife of a President who is chiefly remembered nowadays for having been married to her.

The sweet-faced Mrs. Hayes was honored for her intelligence, beloved for her kind-heartedness (the soldiers who served under her husband's command in the Civil War called her "Mother Lucy" in recognition of the long hours she spent comforting and cheering them) and acclaimed for the refined social skills she demonstrated in the White House. But what particularly endeared her to a large segment of the population was her staunch support for the cause of temperance. She earned the nickname "Lemonade Lucy" for banning liquor from the Executive Mansion, a stand that thrilled those who were convinced that the road to ruin, both personal and national, led through the barroom door.

One such person was Mrs. E. C. Sloan of Baltimore, who sent this earnest letter to Lucretia Garfield in 1881. She writes, she humbly proclaims, "on behalf of suffering humanity" to beg the First Lady to follow the noble example of Mrs. Hayes, "whose fame will resound to the end of time for her firmness in Duty . . . in

banishing the 'Intoxicating Cup' from the 'White House.'" Mrs. Sloan admits that the power of the "Accursed Poison" is formidable, but she is confident that "the time will come when 'Woman' will exterminate Rum, the cause of so much suffering in almost every household. . . ."

Speaking of "Woman," the crusading Mrs. Sloan also wants to know the First Lady's position on female suffrage. She certainly leaves no doubt about her own feelings, calling suffrage "the next needed reform for the perpetuity of good government"; castigating the "'Mass' of illiterate and ignorant men" who are currently running things; and insisting that the "intelligent American woman has more a right in the interest of *her* country than an incompetent and illiterate foreigner." For her to be "deprived of the right of Representation," Mrs. Sloan says, "is injustice in the highest sense."

Whatever her opinions on the subjects of temperance and suffrage, Mrs. Garfield didn't have time to do much about them. Four months after this letter was written, her husband was shot and she had other things on her mind. ✒

254

Boston, Mass. May 11th 1881

Mrs. James R. Garfield,

Dear Madam,—

In looking over the "Herald" this A. M. I noticed that you were ill from nervous prostration, Malaria, &c. &c.

Therefore I write you as one woman to another, believing that if you will use the Electro-magnetic Pad you will thank me for telling you of it. It would take weeks to tell you all they have done for me.

I send you circulars please read them. I will send you a copy of a letter

80699

Mrs. M. A. McMaster *to* Lucretia Garfield

Boston, Massachusetts • May 11, 1881

WHEN MRS. M. A. MCMASTER OF BOSTON READ in the morning newspaper that First Lady Lucretia Garfield was ill with "nervous prostration, malaria &c. &c.," she knew exactly what would restore the President's wife to robust health: an electromagnetic pad. In this letter, the generous lady assures Mrs. Garfield "as one woman to another" that these pads have done her a world of good. "It would take weeks," she writes, "to tell you all they have done for me," neglecting to specify the ailment that afflicted her before these devices made it all better.

She also neglects to mention, though it's spelled out right there in the letterhead, that her husband is manager of the "General Eastern Agency" that sells them.

Lest the First Lady think she's merely plugging her husband's products, the altruistic Mrs. McMaster assures her that she seeks no favors and is "in sympathy with you, on the side of right & justice everywhere." She even encloses a testimonial from a man who works at the American Bank Note Company and is therefore trustworthy. This Mr. Leonard has gained "great benefit" from the wonder-working pads. Again, we are not told exactly what was wrong with him, but he says the pads have helped him gain 15 pounds—something that "the very best Physicians of all the different schools" weren't able to accomplish.

It's unclear whether Mrs. Garfield ever gave the Electro Magnetic Pad a try, but plenty of other people did. Glance through the advertisements in newspapers and magazines of the period and you'll occasionally find, scattered among the breathless paeans to the potency of various tonics and salves and pills, a crude but compelling drawing of people going about their business with electromagnetic belts or pads attached to various parts of their body. To convey a sense of their power, the devices are often shown with jagged rays—like miniature lightning bolts—emanating from them, often right through the wearer's skirts or waistcoat. No wonder they were able to transform users from sickliness to vigor.

Of course it's all very silly, just another laughable example of our ancestors' boundless willingness to believe in just about anything that was touted as a miracle cure.

Or is it? Check the Internet: There are thousands of "magnetic therapy" devices on the market today, and thousands of satisfied customers are prepared to testify to the efficacy of said devices in treating everything from insect bites and PMS to warts and hepatitis C. Magnetic bracelets, rings, knee wraps, belts, quilts, mattress pads, insoles, even pet collars—you name it, it's out there. And if you're worried about magnetic proliferation, you can buy a "Personal Harmoniser" to protect you from harmful electromagnetic radiation. Some users say the optional gold or silver plating strengthens the etheric energy. ❧

Telegram 1

TELEGRAM.

Executive Mansion, 11.40 Am
Washington, D.C. Aug 19. 1881

To Boston Mass
Mrs Garfield
Washn DC

Dear Lady :—
Please apply raw beef steak warmed as poultice to the Prest's stomach & it will restore its tone, renew once an hour also toasted bread soaked in wine

Mons Hunt
8 Auburn St
Charlestown Mass

Telegram 2

TELEGRAM.   192

Executive Mansion,
B&P Dept   Washington, D.C. ____ 188_
Received from July 2. 81   Dated 9.55 Am 188

To Mrs Garfield
Elberon N.J.

The President wishes me to say to you from him that he has been seriously hurt How seriously he cannot yet say. He is himself and hopes you will come to him soon. He sends his love to you

A.F. Rockwell

A. F. Rockwell *to* Lucretia Garfield

Washington, D.C. · July 2, 1881

Moses Hunt *to* Lucretia Garfield

Boston, Massachusetts · August 19, 1881

I N THE SUMMER OF 1881, the steamy weather in Washington was hindering Lucretia Garfield's recuperation from a near-fatal bout of malaria. She went to the seaside resort of Elberon, New Jersey, in search of relief, and it was there that she learned, on July 2, that her husband had been shot in the back as he walked through a railroad station in Washington, D.C. It was the beginning of a long nightmare. ❧ Soon after receiving the bottom telegram shown here, which tells her the President "has been seriously hurt" but "is himself and hopes you will come to him soon," the First Lady rushed

back to Washington, where she spent the following days either sitting beside her husband's bed or preparing his food. At first it seemed he would recover, but then he began to weaken. Infection set in, partly as a result of his doctors' attempts to find and remove the bullet by sticking their unsterilized fingers into the wound. One of them probed so deeply that he actually punctured Garfield's liver.

Alexander Graham Bell took his recently invented metal detector to the White House, but the device had no more success than the doctors in locating the bullet, possibly because the President was lying on a metal bed frame.

Messages of support and advice poured in. The Garfields' nine-year-old son sent a note saying, "I am glad that I am not there because I would only be in the way," adding wistfully, "I suppose you will not have time to write to me." The top telegram shown here urges Mrs. Garfield to apply a poultice of "raw beef steak

warmed" and "toasted bread soaked in wine" to her husband's stomach.

As the temperature soared, it was decided that the fresh sea air of the Jersey shore might be beneficial. After enduring an agonizing journey to Elberon and more probing by his doctors, who by this time had turned a two-inch wound into a suppurating gash that stretched from his groin to his ribcage, Garfield died on September 19, more than two months after being shot and only six months after taking office. Former First Ladies Sarah Polk and Julia Tyler were among those who sent condolences, as was Queen Victoria; it was the second such message she had sent to the White House in just 16 years.

Assassin Charles Guiteau, revealed to be a disappointed office-seeker, was tried, convicted, and hanged. To the end, he insisted—with some justification—that it was the doctors, and not he, who had killed the President. ❧

Lenox Park
Dorsey P.O.
Howard Co.
Md.

Mrs Harrison
                    Dear Madam

I am very sorry you are
sick, so I send you a bird and
couple tomatos hoping you
will enjoy them when you know
that I shot the bird for you
hoping it will do you as
much good as some birds I
shot for a sick lady last
Fall the Doctor said she could
not live but she enjoyed the
bird and is still living.
I would shoot you some partridge but our law is not up
yet, and mama says we must
obey the laws of our state

44061

HOWARD CARTER *to* CAROLINE HARRISON

Dorsey, Maryland • October 1892

FOR MANY AMATEUR STUDENTS OF PRESIDENTIAL HISTORY, the decades after the Civil War are a dimly lit no-man's-land. There's Abraham Lincoln and there's Teddy Roosevelt, but the Presidents in between blur in a sepia-toned parade of stout physiques and facial hair. *Chester Arthur? We didn't really have a President named Chester Arthur, did we? And why is Grover Cleveland listed twice? Must be a typo, right?* ❧ If it's hard to tell one late 19th-century Chief Executive from another, it's even tougher to distinguish among their wives. Take Caroline Harrison, for example. She's almost completely

forgotten today (partly because her reputation has been overshadowed by that of the enormously popular Frances Cleveland, who both preceded and succeeded her in the White House), but in her day she was well liked and well known as a gracious hostess, an accomplished pianist and painter, and a progressive thinker with an interest in improved educational opportunities for women.

Her historical claim to fame rests mainly on three initiatives: She helped found the Daughters of the American Revolution and served as its first president general. She started the famous collection of White House china. And she lobbied hard for a major expansion of the cramped, shabby, rat-infested White House itself. When her efforts failed, she contented herself with buying new furniture, installing electric lights and modern bathrooms, and reportedly bringing in a pack of ferrets to control the rats.

Like a distressing number of First Ladies of the period, Mrs. Harrison had serious health problems. In the fall of 1892, reports of her illness prompted this letter from a young man named Howard

Carter, and doubtless spread panic among the avian population in the vicinity of Dorsey, Maryland. Howard had a gun and a sharp eye, you see, and he liked to shoot birds and present them to ladies who were feeling under the weather.

Calling himself her "little friend," Howard tells Mrs. Harrison that he is sending her a couple of tomatoes he grew and a bird he shot. He wishes it were a partridge, but since it's illegal to shoot them and his mama has raised him to "obey the laws of our state as well as God's laws," Howard has to send "the best I could get." The previous fall, he reports, he shot a bird for another sick lady, and even though "the Doctor said she could not live . . . she enjoyed the bird and is still living."

Sadly, Howard's generous and heartwarming gift didn't work similar wonders for the First Lady, who died of tuberculosis shortly before the end of her husband's single term. We don't know what eventually became of young Master Carter, but the fields and woods where he hunted birds are now part of one of Maryland's fastest growing counties and are being devoured by suburban sprawl. ❧

Pelham Ga.
May 21th 87

Madam Cleveland:

Please pardon
the trespass; As I wish to seek
information concerning your
name, We have a sweet little
boy and girl, who are twins
named for yourself and the
president; Before recording their
names, wish to know whether
or not you have a middle name,
I dont remember to have seen
it given through the press, Also
if you are called Frankie
by those with whom you are connected? Our name is spelled
exactly like that of president
Cleveland, And we desire to give

9800

MRS. G. H. CLEVELAND *to* FRANCES CLEVELAND

Pelham, Georgia • May 21, 1887

I N MANY WAYS, FRANCES CLEVELAND was the Jackie Kennedy of her day. People saw her as a breath of fresh air in the White House—partly because, unlike her matronly predecessors as First Lady, she was young and stylish and strikingly pretty. Her engagement to President Grover Cleveland set tongues wagging over the difference in their ages (she had just finished college, and he was almost three decades older) and the ever-so-slightly-titillating fact that he had helped raise her after the death of her own father (Cleveland's law partner) when she was 11 years old.

Their 1886 wedding in the White House Blue Room—the first, and still the only, presidential wedding in the presidential mansion—set off a turn-of-the-century version of a media frenzy, and the birth of their daughter five years later caused such a sensation that the Curtiss Candy Company claimed to have named the Baby Ruth candy bar after the infant.

In this letter from 1887, a woman in Georgia, obviously relishing the fact that she now shares a famous name, informs Frances Cleveland that she and her husband have named their "sweet little boy and girl, who are twins" after the President and First Lady. Just "Grover" and "Frances" won't do, however, so she asks "whether or not you have a middle name" and wonders whether "you are called Frankie, by those with whom you are acquainted?"

Presumably, the Mrs. Cleveland in the White House told the Mrs. Cleveland in Georgia what she wanted to know: Her middle name was Clara, but she rarely used it. Yes, she was sometimes called "Frankie," but she hated the nickname. Instead, her friends and family, including the President of the United States, called her "Frank." 🐾

Frances Cleveland receives a congratulatory kiss from her mother on her wedding day in 1886.

Carthage Mo
Sep 14. 93

Rather
interesting —
Mrs Cleveland may like

212 West 4 St.

To. Mrs Grover Cleveland.
to read this Washington;
letter. D. C.

Dear Madam.

As there are
so few children of the "White House"
living, I feel that it is an
especial right of mine to send
greetings, and good wishes
of a long, happy, and useful
life to the new baby of the
"White House," and I hope she
may live to send greetings to
some future baby of the "White House"
as I now send mine to her.
As your little girl is now a
White House baby, you may feel
some interest to know a few
facts relating to two other children

29049

SALLY WALKER BOOR *to* FRANCES CLEVELAND

Carthage, Missouri • September 14, 1893

A NAMELESS WHITE HOUSE STAFFER scribbled at the top of the first page, "Mrs Cleveland may like to read this letter." It's a good assessment. If First Lady Frances Cleveland did read this letter, she must have felt a deep sense of connection between herself and those who had occupied the Executive Mansion before her. She may have been the youngest First Lady, but as this letter points out, motherhood had made her part of a long tradition. ❧ On September 9, 1893, Mrs. Cleveland gave birth to a daughter in a second-floor bedroom of the White House. As

the baby girl was the first child of a President born at 1600 Pennsylvania Avenue, her arrival was the subject of rapturous articles in the newspapers of the day. One of those articles caught the eye of a woman in Missouri, who promptly sent this letter to the new mother.

Sally Walker Boor begins by sending "greetings, and good wishes of a long, happy, and useful life" to the infant, who by this time has been named Esther. Then she tells the First Lady about "two other children who were born, lived & played in the White House." One of them, it turns out, is the writer herself, whose father was President James K. Polk's private secretary. "I was born in 1846," she announces with obvious pride, ". . . on Gen'l Jackson's birth-day, and in the room he had occupied." The President wanted to have Sally christened in "a grand affair" at the White House, but the minister informed him that "White House babies . . . must be brought to the Church, just like other babies. Mr. Polk . . . became offended, so my parents, out of respect to him, let the matter rest."

Sally and her brother, who came along in 1847, were members of a select group.

The title of First White House Baby goes to Thomas Jefferson's grandson, born in 1806 while his mother was visiting the capital city. Grandchildren of John Quincy Adams, John Tyler, and Ulysses Grant were born in the White House, as were four children of Andrew Jackson's niece, who also served as the widowed President's official hostess. The most recent birth was that of Woodrow Wilson's grandson, Francis Sayre, Jr., who made his appearance in 1915. Considering the changes in medical practices and cultural attitudes that have taken place since then, it seems likely that there will never be another. A *New York Times* article published at the time of Baby Francis's arrival lists the 11 babies born in the White House over the years—and makes no mention of Sally Walker Boor or her brother.

In her letter, Mrs. Boor expresses the hope that the Clevelands' daughter "may live to send greetings to some future baby of the White House," but it didn't happen. When she died in 1980, Esther Cleveland still held the distinction of being the only presidential child to be born in that great house overlooking Lafayette Square. ❧

11 July '94.

GRAY GABLES.
BUZZARDS BAY,
MASS.

Dear Mr Thurber.

I dont want
by any chance to
have a word of this
get to the President
because he is worried
and anxious enough
but I want to ask
your advice and
assistance. - We have
of course had no
kind of watchman of any
kind here. and we
have been absolutely

30764

Frances Cleveland *to* H. T. Thurber

Buzzards Bay, Massachusetts · July 11, 1894

An unwilling celebrity, Frances Cleveland spent as much time as possible away from the glare of publicity that surrounded the White House. One of the places to which she retreated was Buzzards Bay on Cape Cod, where the Clevelands maintained a summer house called Gray Gables. ❧ The place had much to offer as a vacation spot, including 110 acres of land, a mile-long beach, and its own railroad stop, but perhaps most appealing of all to the Clevelands was the opportunity to live a "normal" life, at least for a while. As the President told a reporter,

"My neighbors are independent, not obtrusively curious, and I only have to behave myself and pay my taxes to be treated like any other citizen. . . ."

Inevitably, the area's atmosphere of restful seclusion began to change. The very presence of the President and his family helped establish Buzzards Bay as a desirable resort, and newcomers started flocking to the place.

More ominously, events in the outside world began to make themselves felt even on remote Cape Cod. In 1894, worsening economic conditions, rising unemployment, and widespread labor unrest led to an increase in threats against the President's life. Finally, a growing sense of unease prompted the First Lady to send this letter to Secret Service official H. T. Thurber.

At Gray Gables, she writes, "We have been absolutely without fear," but now "three different very tough looking men" have been found on the property, and a staff member "had quite a time" getting rid of them. The local authorities are "worried & anxious & think the men are after the children," and the First Lady shares their fears. (She had reason to worry: Glancing out the window one day, she saw a group of sightseers passing one of the children from hand to hand while the nurse looked on helplessly, and on another occasion a visitor tried to snip a lock of Ruth's hair when she passed by.) She asks Thurber "if you might deem it best to have a Secret Service man or Detective sent on to help these local people out."

At the time, protecting the President was not the responsibility of the Secret Service, which had been created to combat counterfeiting. Nonetheless, Frances Cleveland's plea received a prompt and sympathetic response. Even though the action exceeded the agency's mandate, three operatives were quietly assigned to Gray Gables in the summer of 1894, and they returned the following year.

In 1906, Congress officially made the Secret Service responsible for protecting the President; protection was extended to the President's family in 1917. By then, the issue of security at Gray Gables was moot. After 12-year-old Ruth died there of diphtheria in 1904, the grief-stricken Clevelands spent their summers elsewhere. ❧

Market Street,
Oakland.

Mrs. William McKinley.

Dear Madam,

I take the liberty
of sending you a
very necessary sanitary
article for your use
during your illness.
The model of this reseal
is new, but I assure
you will find upon
a trial it a comfort.
I have used a similar
article in my own

MRS. SUSAN WOLFSKILL *to* IDA MCKINLEY

Oakland, California · May 16, 1901

THE WIFE OF OUR 25TH PRESIDENT was one of several 19th-century First Ladies who suffered from poor health. Today, most people know only two things about her: her husband was assassinated, and she was very frail. A website that offers biographical information on her is headed simply "Ida Saxton McKinley: Invalid First Lady." ❦ She grew up in a well-to-do home in Canton, Ohio. Her pretty face and winning personality inspired people to call her "the belle of Canton," while her business acumen was so impressive that her father allowed her to manage the family bank in his absence. When she married a handsome Civil War veteran and aspiring politician named William McKinley, the future looked rosy.

But then Ida's life started spinning out of control. She was diagnosed with phlebitis, which made it difficult to walk or even stand. She was plagued by such blinding headaches that she tried to relieve them by cutting her hair short. Most alarming of all, she started having convulsions. During a three-year period in the 1870s, she lost her beloved mother and two small children; after that, the "fits" came more frequently, and doctors spoke the dreaded word—epilepsy.

Meanwhile, her husband became a prominent public figure, holding a seat in the U.S. House of Representatives for 14 years and serving two terms as governor of Ohio. He never spoke publicly of Ida's condition, but people heard about it anyway and were impressed by his unstinting devotion to his wife.

In 1896, after a spirited campaign conducted almost entirely from his front porch because he didn't want to leave Ida, McKinley was elected President.

In the White House, Ida spent hours knitting thousands of yarn slippers, most of which were donated to the poor. She was often depressed and irritable, but despite the unpredictability of her illness, she refused to ask someone else to act as official hostess. When she attended state dinners, the President violated protocol by insisting that she be seated beside him; if she had a seizure, he covered her face with a handkerchief.

In the spring of 1901, while traveling with her husband, Ida became seriously ill and had to return to Washington. Soon thereafter, a woman in California sent her this letter and a surprising gift. With the utmost delicacy, the writer describes it only as "a very necessary sanitary article." Having used one herself, she is sure that it will be "a comfort" to the First Lady. A staff member's handwritten notation tells us that it's a "side bed-pan."

We don't know whether Ida ever used the "vessel," but a few weeks later she felt well enough to join the President on another trip, this time to visit the Pan-American Exposition in Buffalo. ❦

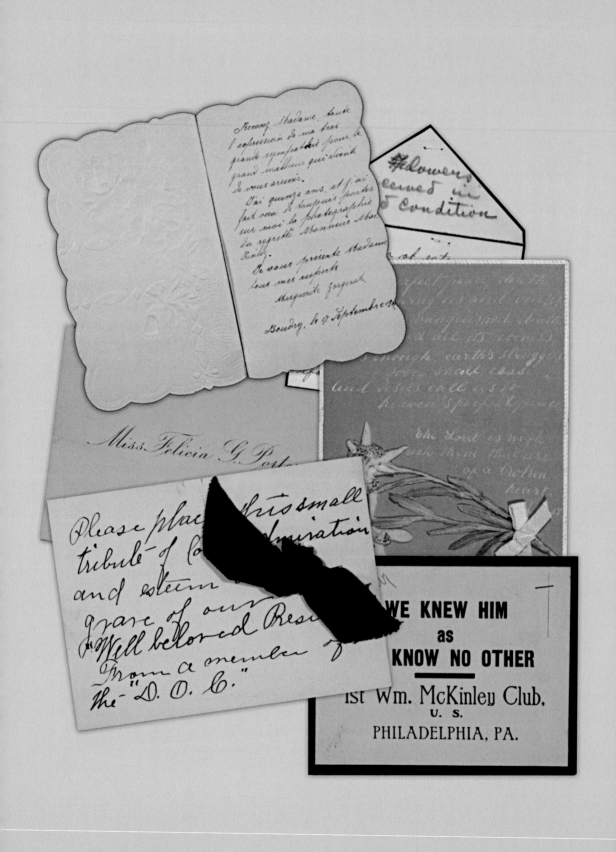

Recevez Madame, toute
l'expression de ma très
grande sympathie pour le
grand malheur qui vient
de vous arriver.

J'ai quinze ans, et j'ai
fait voir la toujours porté
sur moi la photographie
du regretté Monsieur Mac
Kinley.

Je vous présente Madame
tous mes respects

Marguerite Gorgerat.

Boudry, le 17 Septembre 1901

#dowens
received in
Condition

Miss Felicia G. Porter

Please place this small
tribute of love admiration
and esteem on the
grave of our
Well beloved President
From a member of
the "D. O. C."

WE KNEW HIM
as
KNOW NO OTHER

1st Wm. McKinley Club,
U. S.
PHILADELPHIA, PA.

Various Writers *to* Ida McKinley

Addresses Unknown • September 1901

PRESIDENT McKINLEY HAD ORIGINALLY PLANNED to attend the opening of the Pan-American Exposition in May 1901, but his wife's illness forced him to postpone the trip. When he finally went to Buffalo early in September, Ida accompanied him. ❧ On September 6, the McKinleys spent the morning at Niagara Falls; in the afternoon, the First Lady rested while her husband attended a reception at the exposition's Temple of Music. Unnoticed among the hundreds of people who lined up to shake the President's hand, a young anarchist named Leon Czolgosz made his way through

the crowd of well-wishers and calmly shot McKinley in the stomach. When aide George Cortelyou rushed to the President's side, the wounded man's first words were, "My wife, Cortelyou—be careful how you tell her."

Like Garfield some 20 years earlier, McKinley at first seemed likely to survive but eventually succumbed to infection. Having stayed with him almost continuously for a week while he clung to life, Ida was at his bedside when he died quietly on September 14.

A huge outpouring of grief followed the announcement of the President's death. He had been in office almost five years, had led the country through a triumphant war with Spain that made the United States a true world power, and was universally regarded as an honest, decent, trustworthy man. One eulogist said that McKinley's life exhibited "every phase of the best and noblest attributes of human character." Another said simply, "He was really the idol of the nation." Many heaped special praise on him for the loving care he had given to his invalid wife.

Shown here is a small sample of the thousands of tokens of sympathy that were sent to the First Lady. Not shown is a handwritten note, accompanied by a modest bouquet, that reflects the nation's pain: "May the little rose be placed in the casket at the feet of our noble Chieftain as a simple loving token from a deeply grieved Southern heart loyal to him." ❧

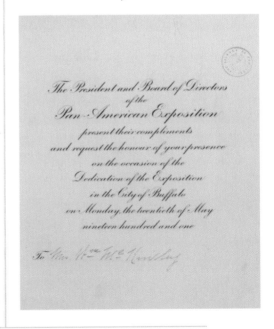

Mrs. McKinley's invitation to the opening of the Pan American Exposition in Buffalo, New York

Oyster Bay, N. Y.
September 18, 1902.

Dear Mr. McKim:

I have marked the chintz that we prefer, and have returned the others to you by express to-day.

I do not like my writing desk at all. I think it ought to be made to match the furniture which is rosewood, carved with big birds, I should say about fifty years old. Perhaps it would be a good thing to have a photograph taken of the bed. In any case I think the drawing of the writing table is ugly and inconvenient. About the blue room samples, before deciding I would like to know how the room is to be decorated, whether the silk is for covering furniture or hanging on the walls, or whether you mean to use blue and gold brocade with it, like the old sample. My daughter and I are rather converted to your dark blue, but the President still thinks it would make an ugly evening room, so to satisfy him I would like to know exactly how you propose it should look completed. I have kept

Edith Roosevelt *to* Charles F. McKim

Oyster Bay, New York • September 18, 1902

FIRST LADY EDITH ROOSEVELT HAD HER HANDS FULL IN 1902. She had a husband whose zest for life led a friend to remark, "You must always remember that the President is about six." She had six children whose rambunctious antics were never-ending: The youngest, Quentin, once took a pony upstairs to cheer a sick brother, and the oldest, Alice, kept a garter snake in her purse to startle unwary guests. And she had a household in chaos as the White House underwent its first complete renovation since the fire of 1814. ❧ There had been talk of constructing a new Executive Mansion on another site, but the President wouldn't hear of it. Instead, renowned architect Charles F. McKim was charged with giving the historic building a complete makeover. While Edith and the children relaxed on Long Island and the President occupied a house on Lafayette Square, gangs of workmen created bedrooms in the White House attic, enlarged the State Dining Room, relocated the main staircase, built a brand-new West Wing, and replaced Victorian clutter with neo-Georgian serenity.

By the time Edith wrote this letter to McKim, final design details were being settled. She approves some fabric samples, tells the architect that she and her daughter are "rather converted" to the color he proposes for the Blue Room, and minces no words in her opinion of the design for a new writing desk, which she finds "ugly and inconvenient." Against McKim's wishes, the President had insisted on retaining a mid-19th-century bedroom suite, and Edith wants the desk redesigned to match the older pieces. McKim must have shuddered at the thought of desecrating his rooms with old-fashioned furniture of "rosewood, carved with big birds," but he complied with the request. ❧

Charles Bittinger captures the interior design of the White House's Blue Room as it was in 1903.

Sunday.
April 26, 1903.

Dear Mother,

I got the water pistol it came through without getting caught, but all the chocolate and guava jelly got caught, one of the best reasons why it got caught was because the box was marked Huylas so of course the looked in. The water pistol is just the right kind, I didn't want to bother you by explaining about the kind, but if I had explained it would have been just the kind. I have had great fun with it both mornings since I got it. I went in and woke boys up by pouring it down their necks when they were asleep. This morning I had a duel with another boy we each got behind our curtains and fired at each other. How we escaped without getting caught I don't know, but we did.

Philip Christie, Pleface Amory, Sargent and myself are making a hut we started it this morning we put a broken down tree on two trees like this

Tree   Tree

and thatched the sides with pine branches, it was an awful job but we have got it nearly all done.

Yesterday we played the Brown College Sophmores and beat the 14 to 9.

Your loving
Kermit.

KERMIT ROOSEVELT *to* EDITH ROOSEVELT

Address Unknown • April 26, 1903

I T TAKES A SPECIAL KIND OF MOTHER TO SMUGGLE a water pistol to her son at boarding school, so we have to conclude that 13-year-old Kermit had the *best mom ever.* ❧ Detailing not only Kermit's prowess with the water pistol but also his participation in the construction of a fine thatched hut, this letter is typical of the correspondence that passed between the high-spirited boy and his doting mother. In a later example, Edith asks Kermit whether his new trousers have arrived and reminds him to write his name on them, tells him about

some minor surgery on the President's leg ("he only had to have cocaine"), and wishes he could have joined her to see *The Defender* ("You know it has 'She's my tootsey-wootsey' . . . in it"). It's all very maternal and ordinary—except for the fact that Edith's stationery is headed "White House, Washington."

After a somewhat delicate childhood, Kermit embraced the Roosevelt doctrine of The Strenuous Life. As a freshman at Harvard, he accompanied his father on an African safari, then completed his studies in only two and a half years. In 1914, his heroic efforts saved TR's life after the former President developed malaria on a harrowing expedition through the Amazon jungle. After serving in World War I, he enjoyed a successful business career and wrote several books about his exploits as a hunter and explorer.

Years of drinking too much and living too hard left him unfit for frontline combat in World War II. Assigned to out-of-the-way Fort Richardson, Alaska, he went into his room one evening and shot himself.

Edith Roosevelt was told that her son had died of a heart attack. ❧

Frances Benjamin Johnston captured this image of Kermit Roosevelt with his dog, Jack, in June 1902.

Hazardous!

Friday, 1st June, 1906.

My dear Mrs Roosevelt:

Alma Tadema, the artist, told me the other evening a little story about Winston Churchill's encounter with one of his brother artists which may interest you.

As Tadema told it, the artist was making a little sketch of a group of noted people gathered at some social occasion. The sketch was intended for publication, and Winston was not one of those to be included. He thought it a good group to be in, however, and kept hovering about it and putting himself under the artist's eye until the latter rather in self-defense sketched him in slightly in profile in the outer line.

When the sketch was finished they were all crowding around to look at it and expressing, as is apt to be the case at such times, favorable opinions of the artist's work. Winston, having got into the picture in this fashion came up to give his opinion, and in his characteristic way said: "I don't agree with you. I don't think the likenesses are good at all. Look at that thing of me. Surely that isn't like me." The artist, whom Tadema described as one of the most patient and gentle spoken of his race, turned at this like the proverbial worm. "Yes," he said. "I think you are right,Mr. Churchill. It doesn't do you full justice, but then you see it is in profile, so that I could only get in half your cheek."

Any little story like this against Winston is received with delight

WHITELAW REID *to* EDITH ROOSEVELT

London, England · June 1, 1906

IN THE COURSE OF A LONG AND DISTINGUISHED CAREER, Whitelaw Reid served as American ambassador to France (1889-92) and Great Britain (1905-12) and was the Republican candidate for Vice President in 1892. He also made a name for himself as a journalist, working as a reporter during the Civil War and later succeeding Horace Greeley as editor of the *New York Tribune,* and as the author of several well-received volumes of American history and authoritative discourses on foreign affairs. ❧ Besides these impeccable professional credentials, Reid possessed

a couple of other gifts that made him a highly valued correspondent: He was an entertaining raconteur and, perhaps more important, an avid gossip. During his tenure at the Court of St. James's, he sent official reports to President Roosevelt on a regular basis, and at some point he began sending long letters to First Lady Edith Roosevelt as well, offering an insider's view of goings-on among the members of the diplomatic corps and the highest levels of English society. Which prominent personage has "taken to drink," which wife of a famous figure is in such bad health that she "has to be placed in the carriage as if she were a baby," which royal prince is slightly deaf and has a glass eye, which "substantial English matron" curtsied too deeply and almost didn't get up again—Reid spilled the beans on all of them in letters like this one from 1906.

Appropriately headed "Hazardous!" and running on for an amazing 21 pages, the letter begins with an anecdote about Winston Churchill, who at the time was the 31-year-old undersecretary of state for the colonies. Reid notes that such unflattering

stories are always "received with delight in London" because no one is "more thoroughly . . . detested in the more important social circles" than Churchill, partly because in 1904 he had switched his party affiliation from Conservative to Liberal and was therefore considered something of a traitor to his class.

The King's sister apparently spoke for many others when she whispered to Reid one evening, "I mustn't say it publicly, but I detest him." Given our image of the bulldog-like Churchill as one of the towering figures of modern times, it is startling to find the ambassador referring to him archly as "this boy," just as it is hard not to chuckle at the prediction that Churchill might wind up like his father, who died (of syphilis, according to rumor) at the age of 45.

Reid's letters were so popular that he was later encouraged to send similar missives to First Lady Helen Taft. Just as we thrive on a steady diet of celebrity gossip today, inquiring minds a century ago also wanted the lowdown on the upper crust—and Whitelaw Reid was only too happy to provide it. ❧

Beverly—

My dear Will—

      I am tolerably
well—you see how I take
to this word—And pretty
comfortable—I do not
like this thing of being
silent, but I dont know
what to do about it—
      The doctor insists that
I will get well, and

HELEN TAFT *to* WILLIAM HOWARD TAFT

Beverly, Massachusetts · 1909

APHASIA. THE DICTIONARY DEFINES IT as "the loss of ability to understand or express speech," but dry words can't begin to convey the catastrophic reality of this sudden insult to the body and mind. First Lady Helen Taft knew all about aphasia, and she didn't like it one bit. ❧ On May 17, 1909, just two months after her husband's Inauguration, Mrs. Taft suffered a stroke that left the left side of her body paralyzed and robbed her of the ability to speak. In this letter written from the seaside town of Beverly, Massachusetts, where the Tafts maintained a

summer home, the First Lady's frustration and worry are palpable.

In what may be an attempt to put up a cheerful front for her husband's sake, she tells him that she is "tolerably well . . . and pretty comfortable." With a mixture of hope and resignation, she repeats a comment from her doctor, who "insists that I will get well, and says that it is a long time to do so." Her aggravation is most evident in a single sentence: "I do not like this thing of being silent, but I don't know what to do about it."

The enforced silence must have been particularly hard for a well-educated, vigorous, articulate woman like Nellie Taft. In 1900, she happily followed her husband to the Philippines after he was appointed governor of the newly acquired islands, and soon after their return to Washington in 1903 she set her sights on the White House. Critics have claimed that she nagged the affable Taft into the Presidency when what he really wanted was to be a justice of the Supreme Court.

The charge is probably an exaggeration, but the unabashedly ambitious Mrs. Taft did assume a vigorous role (she called

it "an active interest") in securing Theodore Roosevelt's support for her husband's nomination. During her first few weeks as First Lady she made several changes in the running of the Executive Mansion and demonstrated her interest in improving working conditions for federal employees, but then came the stroke. And the silence.

During his wife's recuperation, the President encouraged Whitelaw Reid to write to her as he had to Edith Roosevelt. Ambassador Reid's gossipy letters from London doubtless helped pass the time for Nellie, but it was her strong will and tireless determination that pulled her through the strenuous, year-long period of rehabilitation.

Though she eventually regained the ability to talk, the effects of the stroke remained visible in a shuffling gait and a speech that was sometimes hard for strangers to understand. She was unable to play the active role in her husband's administration that she probably would have wished, and some say that Taft's failure to win reelection in 1912 was at least partly due to the fact that Nellie wasn't there to push him. ❧

113 Ridge St., N.Y. City
March 9, 1916

From an humble and heartbroken mother to the
Hon. Mrs. William H. Taft

Dear Madam,

I address
this letter to you because all else has
failed. I have a son, Solomon Schein,
eleven years old, who, until recently was
in Europe with my father. Now, my
father died and my child was left alone
without any one to take care of him.

My husband, a citizen of the
United States, brought him to this country
from Europe, but the immigration officials
at Ellis Island refuse to admit him

3180

Mrs. Pincus Schein *to* Helen Taft

New York, New York • March 9, 1910

WHEN A LETTER BEGINS, "I address this letter to you because all else has failed," you know it isn't good news. ❧ Toward the end of the 19th century, a huge and growing flood of immigrants to the United States was utterly transforming the ethnic makeup of American society, convincing many uneasy people of the need to rethink—and maybe withdraw—the Statue of Liberty's invitation to send this country "the wretched refuse of your teeming shore." The result of these fears was a string of increasingly restrictive immigration laws, most of them intended to ensure

that America remained predominantly white, gentile, and Protestant. First, immigration of Chinese laborers was severely restricted, then banned altogether. Within a few years, the roster of so-called undesirables prohibited from entering the country was expanded to include polygamists, the mentally ill, anyone convicted of a crime "involving moral turpitude," anyone likely to become a "public charge," and persons suffering from a "loathsome disease."

This is the net that snared an 11-year-old boy named Solomon Schein in 1910. He was in Europe with his grandfather when the old man died. Solomon's father, a U.S. citizen, brought him home, but officials at Ellis Island classified the "badly tongue-tied" boy as an "idiot" and refused to admit him. Those are the bare facts. Much more is implied but unspoken: the terror the boy must have suffered in the echoing hall at Ellis Island, the anguish of the father who had recently lost a parent and now might lose a son as well, the increasingly desperate visits to the offices of implacable bureaucrats that the mother must have endured before deciding that her last, best hope lay in writing to the First Lady.

In her heartrending letter, Mrs. Schein appeals repeatedly to Helen Taft's maternal instincts, noting that she has children of her own "and can feel with me," then driving the point home by referring to herself as "an humble and heartbroken mother," "a stricken mother," and "a mother in suspense and anguish." Little Solomon, she concludes poignantly, has already "borne more than is allotted to one of his age" and should not be forced to suffer the additional trauma of "solitary desertion among a mass of strangers."

Happily for Mrs. Schein, writing to the First Lady—especially a First Lady like Helen Taft—was the right thing to do. Mrs. Taft promptly intervened in the matter of young Solomon Schein. We don't know what she said to the federal officials involved, but her argument appears to have been extremely persuasive. On March 15, 1910, the President received this message from Secretary of Commerce and Labor Charles Nagel: "We have concluded to direct the admission of the boy. The case is one of unusual hardship, and the family has Mrs. Taft to thank for the decision." ❧

My dear Mrs Ozaki

I received your very
interesting letter, describing how the
Cherry trees came to Washington. And
I am delighted to hear that the Mayor
of Tokio, my remarks were responsible
for it the beautiful gift — I planted
fifty the first year and fifty the
next year — in the outer part of the
Park, so I thought it was, that planting
that made the Mayor of Tokio send them —
and am delighted to hear the truth at last —
— I am very sorry to hear of your
illness — and hope you are getting
well now — I am so glad that you
and your husband are coming
to Washington later — I will be
with warmest remembrances —

HELEN TAFT *to* MADAME YUKIO OZAKI

Washington, D.C. • Date Unknown

THROUGH QUIET PERSUASION AND ENERGETIC ACTION, First Ladies have left their mark on the landscape of Washington in a variety of ways, from improving housing conditions to spearheading the preservation of Lafayette Square. In terms of visual impact, few have created a more enduring legacy than Helen Taft, who planted a bit of Japan on the banks of the Potomac. ❧ Mrs. Taft had lived in Japan, so she didn't need much convincing when a Washington woman named Eliza Scidmore wrote to her in 1909, suggesting that Japanese flowering cherry trees be planted on the newly reclaimed parkland along the Potomac. The First Lady saw to the purchase and planting of 90 trees, and in a remarkably generous gesture, the city of Tokyo donated 2,000 more. Then disaster struck: The donated trees were found to be diseased and had to be burned. When Tokyo Mayor Yukio Ozaki learned that his gift had gone awry, he quickly rounded up a new shipment of trees— more than 3,000 this time. The First Lady and the Japanese ambassador's wife planted the first two of them on March 27, 1912, in a ceremony that marked the humble beginning of today's Cherry Blossom Festival.

In this undated letter, Mrs. Taft thanks Ozaki's wife for having written an insider's account of "how the cherry trees came to Washington." The First Lady's description of her own contribution—"I planted fifty the first year, and fifty the next year"—summarizes a beautification project that has become a living symbol of international friendship. On a visit to Washington in 1950, just five years after the United States and Japan had been bitter enemies, former mayor Ozaki wrote a poem about the blossoms' power to soothe the spirit and help heal the wounds of war. It begins, "Am I awake or do I dream, so generous the welcome here. . . ." ❧

Robert Latou Dickinson's 1918 drawing shows the Tidal Basin's famous blooming cherry trees.

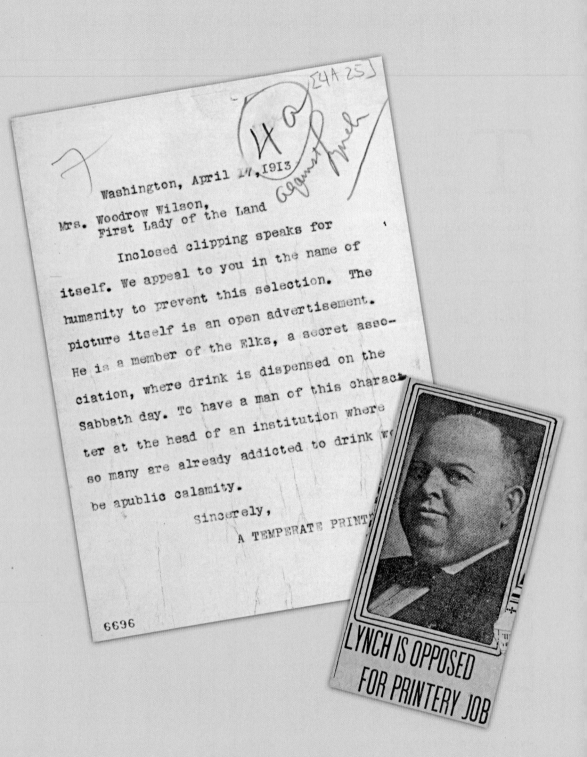

Washington, April 17, 1913

Mrs. Woodrow Wilson,
First Lady of the Land

Inclosed clipping speaks for
itself. We appeal to you in the name of
humanity to prevent this selection. The
picture itself is an open advertisement.
He is a member of the Elks, a secret association, where drink is dispensed on the
Sabbath day. To have a man of this character at the head of an institution where
so many are already addicted to drink wo
be apublic calamity.

Sincerely,
A TEMPERATE PRINT

6696

LYNCH IS OPPOSED
FOR PRINTERY JOB

A TEMPERATE PRINTER *to* ELLEN WILSON

Washington, D.C. · *April 17, 1913*

THE PHRASE "TEMPERANCE MOVEMENT," conjuring images of a phalanx of stern women marching under the leadership of interesting figures such as "Lemonade Lucy" Hayes and Carry Nation, is most often associated with the reform crusades of the Victorian era. In fact, the movement retained its strength well into the 20th century, culminating in the passage of the 18th Amendment and the imposition of Prohibition. As this letter demonstrates, temperance was certainly an emotionally charged issue in 1913. ❧ People have always tried to invoke the First Lady's assistance in securing or

preventing appointments to federal office. In 1913, the important position of public printer—a low-key title for the head of the Government Printing Office, which prints everything from tax returns to passports—became vacant. When word got out that President Woodrow Wilson's likely choice for the job was James M. Lynch, president of the International Typographical Union, alarm bells went off in the minds of many people, and lots of them quickly reached for a pen and paper and started composing letters to the White House.

Opponents of his appointment found a lot to dislike in Mr. Lynch. According to a newspaper article of the period, Democrats claimed that his loyalty to the party was weak, nonunion workers in the Government Printing Office feared that he would require every employee to have a union card, and proud professional printers bemoaned the fact that he had been "out of the actual work of printing for a number of years."

The unnamed writer of this letter, a self-styled proponent of temperance, points out that Lynch is "a member of the Elks, a secret association, where drink is dispensed

on the Sabbath day" and appeals to Mrs. Wilson "in the name of humanity" (First Ladies get lots of appeals couched in those terms) to prevent such a man from becoming head of—*gasp!*—"an institution where so many are already addicted to drink."

Others who wrote to Ellen Wilson were more concerned about Lynch's religion than his alleged fondness for alcohol. One correspondent, calling herself "a good Presbyterian" like Mrs. Wilson and fearing that her letter "might never pass beyond the hands of a Catholic secretary," informed the First Lady that "the Gov't Printing Office is considered already to be in control of the Catholics," and Lynch's appointment would only make a deplorable situation worse. Another, claiming that his opinion "should at least have a little weight" because he had been a printer for 40 years, bluntly described Lynch as "a Romanist, a worshipper of the Tyrant upon the Tiber."

Regardless of whether the Government Printing Office really was the iniquitous den of drunkards and papists that its critics claimed, and whether letters like these had any influence, Mr. Lynch didn't get the job. ❧

2143 - N - Street
Washington, D. C.

September 25, 1913,

My dear Mrs Wilson,

Since the enclosed
bill was introduced, Mr
Borland has referred a number of people (reporters and
others) to me for particulars
about it because I drew it
up, and they have almost
invariably asked — "Is Mrs
Wilson in favor of it?"
To which I have been
obliged to answer, "I do

EDITH E. WOOD *to* ELLEN WILSON

Washington, D.C. • September 25, 1913

AFTER YEARS OF HARD WORK, housing expert Edith E. Wood has finally secured the introduction of a bill in Congress that would improve living conditions for thousands of Washington residents. But when she talks to people about the proposed law, they always ask, "Is Mrs. Wilson in favor of it?" In this letter, she poses the question to Mrs. Wilson herself. ✺ In the early decades of the 20th century, so-called alley housing—a reference to the fact that substandard dwellings were crowded into filthy, narrow alleys all over the city—was the shame of the nation's capital.

First Lady Ellen Wilson became an outspoken advocate of eliminating this slum housing, even leading tours of the alleys to show how squalid they were, so the answer to Edith Wood's question was easy: *Yes*, Mrs. Wilson was emphatically in favor of a law to eliminate alley dwellings.

Mrs. Wilson died less than a year after this letter was written, but her deathbed plea may have helped spur congressional action. A few deteriorated houses were demolished, but two world wars and the Great Depression intervened, and it wasn't until the 1950s that large numbers of alley dwellings were razed and replaced by new public-housing projects. One of them, not far from the Capitol, was named Ellen Wilson Dwellings in honor of the crusading First Lady. In a sadly ironic twist, it deteriorated into an ugly, crime-ridden slum and was demolished in the 1990s. ✺

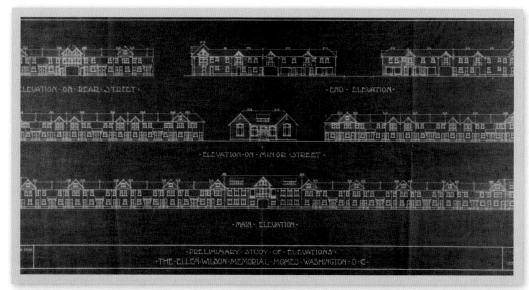

Architects drew up these blueprints in 1915 for "Ellen Wilson Memorial Homes," apartments in Washington, D.C.

My Darling,

Whenever I fail to live up to the great standards which your dear love has set for me a passion of sorrow and remorse sweeps over me which my self-control cannot always withstand

Your own Woodrow

I love you! I love you. I love you.

W.

With tender love to the loveliest lady in the world. W.   18 Dec. '15

The President

WOODROW WILSON *to* EDITH WILSON

Washington, D.C. • *December 18, 1915*

Washington, D.C. • *1921*

FIRST LADY ELLEN WILSON DIED of a chronic kidney ailment known as Bright's disease in the summer of 1914. Seven months later, the grief-stricken President received what he called "a gift from heaven" in the form of an attractive, charming widow named Edith Galt. They met at the White House, where Edith was visiting a friend who was also the President's cousin. Edith's shoes were muddy that day and she feared she didn't look her best, but Wilson, who once confessed "a pretty girl is my chief pleasure," apparently thought she looked just fine. ❧ Soon they were sharing romantic dinners and long drives in the presidential Pierce-Arrow. He sent her orchids and passionate letters—sometimes three or four a day—that belie our one-dimensional image of Wilson as a prim scholar. Only two months after they met, he wrote of his longing for the day when Edith's "dear, beautiful form" would be "close beside me and I . . . have only to stretch out my arms to have [you] come to them . . . my kisses on [your] lips and eyelids. . . ." He often addressed her as "little girl," and on at least one occasion he signed himself "Tiger."

Predictably, the romance was a hot topic for gossip. Some said it was unseemly for Wilson to be courting so soon after his wife's death, and others maintained that the President should stick to the business of running the country. In one of his letters to Edith, Wilson described the strain of being discreet in public: "If ever again I have to be with you for an hour and a half with only two stolen glances to express my all but irresistible desire to take you in my arms and smother you with kisses, I am sure I shall crack an artery!"

He proposed to her on the moonlit White House portico, and they were married on December 18, 1915, at Edith's home in Washington. On their wedding day, Edith received this card, its handwritten message offering a tender contrast to the formal engraved inscription. The second note, written in 1921, shows that six years of marriage had not dampened Wilson's ardor. We don't know what prompted him to write, but it appears that something has made him feel "a passion of sorrow and remorse" for having failed to measure up to the "great standards" set by Edith's love. He closes with a heartfelt declaration—in triplicate.

A single snapshot illustrates love's effect on Wilson: As the honeymoon train sped toward The Homestead resort in Virginia in 1915, a Secret Service agent reportedly stumbled upon the unsettling spectacle of the President of the United States dancing a jig and singing "Oh, you beautiful doll." ❧

(COPY)

Birmingham, Ala.

Apr. 10th, 1917.

Sec. of Interior,

    Washington, D. C.

Hon. Sir:

    I am a descendant of P
Wilson married Mrs. Galt, nee Mi
of Pocahontas and Powhatan, als
family history, notwithstanding
not to publish a poem about the
not know your name, but Judge
Wilson has broken the greatest
and liquors to Mrs. Wilson, an
shall <u>give</u>, or <u>treat</u> or bootle
and ect. You can read it you

    Now Sec. of Interi
Woodrow Wilson's arrest immed
States of America at once. I
as I was given you two as th
prosecution at once. Please
and have it put into effect
Judge Price Williams of Mob
have sat on Bench so long h
to represent my side at the

Respt.

Mrs. May H. Gonzalez.

THE SECRETARY OF THE INTERIOR
WASHINGTON

Dear Mrs Wilson.

Here is a letter that places a terrible power in my hands. If at any time you wish this power exercised I shall not hesitate to do my duty.

Yours for the Enforcement of law

May Gonzalez *to* Franklin K. Lane

Birmingham, Alabama · April 10, 1917

Franklin K. Lane *to* Edith Wilson

Washington, D.C. · Date Unknown

G OVERNMENT SERVICE IS SERIOUS BUSINESS, but it isn't an endless treadmill of protocol and dull routine. Once in a while, things lighten up. �&ue; In the tumultuous spring of 1917, just a few days after the United States formally entered World War I, Secretary of the Interior Franklin K. Lane received this unusual letter from a woman in Alabama named May Gonzalez. Knowing that the First Lady is a descendant of Pocahontas (a fact of which she was very proud), and knowing also that Mrs. Wilson takes a drink now and then, Mrs. Gonzalez reminds Lane that

"the law says no one shall give, or treat or bootleg or sell . . . liquor to an Indian," which means that President Wilson has broken "the greatest law" of the land by serving alcoholic beverages to his wife. The whistle-blower's instructions are clear: "I wish you to get out a warrant for President Woodrow Wilson's arrest immediately according to the laws of these United States of America at once."

The obvious question is, was Mrs. Gonzalez serious? Did she actually expect the nation's Chief Executive to be arrested? Was the letter just a joke, or an attempt (albeit a clumsy one) to embarrass President and Mrs. Wilson?

In any case, Lane forwarded the letter to the First Lady. Bemoaning the fact that the letter "places a terrible power in my hands," he solemnly—and, presumably, with tongue firmly planted in cheek— informs Mrs. Wilson, "If at any time you wish this power exercised, I shall not hesitate to do my duty."

Demonstrating the easy relationship she enjoyed with many members of the Cabinet, Edith penned a prompt and witty response. She has read the letter to her husband, she writes, "& he insists that he thinks the law she speaks of applies only to those of my tribe living on a Reservation & is not applicable to us when we are at large." Noting that "the accused is now performing patriotic service," she thinks it best "that he be warned against further offense—and that we hold this weapon given into our hand for future use should he become irresponsible."

The bantering exchange is a semi-comic echo of Wingematub's pleading letter to Harriet Lane in 1858. It is pleasant to imagine the President and his wife enjoying a quiet laugh over the whole silly affair. Having just committed the nation to a bloody war he had once claimed to be "too proud to fight," Wilson didn't have many occasions for mirth that spring. �&ue;

THE WHITE HOUSE
WASHINGTON

18 December, 1919

Dear Mrs. Wilson:

    Please don't think I am trying to crowd you or to urge im-

mediate action by the President, but I thought it would help you if

you could have before you a list of matters that at intervals the

President might wish to have presented to him for discussion and

settlement.

    I submit such a list, as follows:

✓ Message as to railroads, if any.

    Recognition of Costa Rica.

/ . Selection of commission to settle miners' strike.

    Appointments as follows:

    B   Secretaryship of the Treasury.

    Secretaryship of the Interior.

    Assistant Secretaryship of Agriculture.

    Action upon Secretary Lansing's recommendation of William
        Phillips for Holland.

    Oklahoma appointments recommended by the Attorney General,
        now before the President. (The President has ob-
        jected to these because of his desire to know
        whether Senator Gore approved these appointments.
        I took the matter up with Senator Owen and he says
        they are friends of his and not of Gore's and he
        desires the President to okeh them.)

Joseph P. Tumulty *to* Edith Wilson

Washington, D.C. · *December 18, 1919*

EDITH WILSON HAS BEEN CALLED THE FIRST FEMALE PRESIDENT, and this remarkable letter helps us see why. ❦ At the end of World War I, President Wilson's lofty vision of a fair and democratic postwar world led many people to hail him as the savior of Western civilization. But the acclaim soon dissolved in bitterness: At the 1919 Paris peace conference, wrangling among the Allies doomed many of Wilson's proposals, and opponents in Congress fought adamantly against American participation in the League of Nations. ❦ Desperate to win

public support for his cherished League, Wilson undertook a rigorous cross-country speaking tour that ended in sudden tragedy: After traveling 8,000 miles and delivering dozens of speeches, he collapsed and had to be rushed back to Washington. A few days later he suffered a stroke that left him partially paralyzed and barely able to see.

Immediately, the First Lady and the President's personal physician, Dr. Cary Grayson, erected an impenetrable wall around the stricken man's sickroom. Occasional bulletins assured the public that all was well, and an elaborate charade was staged to show some suspicious members of Congress that Wilson—propped in a chair in a semidarkened room—was on the mend. White House usher Ike Hoover later offered his assessment of the President's true condition: "All his natural functions had to be artificially assisted and he appeared just as helpless as one could possibly be and live."

Rumors began to circulate that the First Lady was actually running the country, telling the President what to sign and even making decisions in his

name. The extent to which Edith actually wielded executive power may never fully be known, but her complete control over the flow of information to and from her husband is evident in this letter from Joseph Tumulty, the President's secretary. It offers a lengthy list of pressing matters, ranging from the recognition of a new government in Costa Rica to the filling of vacancies in the Cabinet and the diplomatic corps, that need to be presented to Wilson "for discussion and settlement." Presumably, the First Lady guided (and perhaps influenced) the discussion, and her handwritten notes appear to indicate that she chose not to bother the President with matters that she considered unimportant.

Wilson managed to serve out the remainder of his term and died, a frail and bitterly disappointed man, in 1924. In her memoir, published several years later, Edith insisted that she had done no more than her wifely duty: "Woodrow Wilson was first my beloved husband whose life I was trying to save, fighting with my back against the wall—after that he was President of the United States." ❦

August 25, 1923.

Dear Evalyn:

I was so glad to get your telegram
and to know you had arrived safely and
had found the children all well. Of
course I miss you but I am getting on
very well, with days full of looking
over my papers and repacking some of my
things. I have only been able to walk
in the grounds once for about ten minutes
but can't begin to tell you how much I
enjoy the porch upstairs. I am out there
most of the day and manage to do a lot
of work in that way out of doors. The
Coolidges and the Cabinet have been out
to see me, and I had a long and interesting talk the other day with
Mr. Charles Warren about Mexico. I
think of you all many times a day, and
want you to please know of my gratitude
for all your wonderful thoughtfulness.
It does help me to carry my burden, as
much as is possible, to live in such an
environment. The grounds are so beautiful and it is all so peaceful that it
must inspire the beautiful thoughts I
need to help me.

With much love to you and Ned and
the dear children, I am

Affectionately yours,

Florence Kling Harding

FLORENCE HARDING *to* EVALYN MCLEAN

Washington, D.C. • *August 25, 1923*

FLORENCE HARDING'S DETRACTORS PAINT HER as a nagging wife who pushed her husband into a job for which he was uniquely unsuited and who may even have murdered him when his indiscretions began to come to light. ❧ Others, however, insist that Mrs. Harding was the paradigm of the modern woman—a gutsy divorcée who ran a newspaper, engaged the services of movie stars for the 1920 presidential campaign, and engineered her husband's elevation to the White House. ❧ After Harding's Inauguration, Florence reportedly said to him, "Well, Warren Harding,

I've given you the Presidency—now what are you going to do with it?" What he did was turn it into a reeking morass of malfeasance. His attorney general was tried twice for corruption, his interior secretary became the first Cabinet member to be imprisoned, and his director of the Veterans Bureau was so outrageously dishonest that Harding once tried to strangle him. While the President engaged in a string of dalliances, including one tryst

in an Oval Office closet, the First Lady flouted Prohibition by serving cocktails to his poker-playing cronies.

Florence's best friend was Evalyn Walsh McLean, wife of the publisher of the *Washington Post* and owner of the Hope Diamond. After President Harding died suddenly on August 2, 1923—felled, according to various reports and rumors, by a heart attack, a meal of tainted crab, or a dose of poison—Evalyn invited her widowed friend to use the McLeans' Washington estate, known as Friendship, as a temporary retreat. Florence took several crates of government documents with her to Friendship, where she systematically (and illegally) destroyed those she considered incriminating.

In this black-bordered letter to Evalyn, written three weeks after Harding's death, Florence refers innocuously to "days full of looking over my papers" at Friendship. Her efforts to protect her husband's reputation failed: Harding is generally considered the worst President in history. ❧

Evalyn McLean and Florence Harding, robed in 1920s finery, were fast friends through difficult times.

Washington
July Eighth
Nineteen Hundred
Twenty Four

File
FLB
per
JB

The Korean people learn with deepest sorrow of your bereavement and humbly beg of you to accept their sincere sympathy, their condolence and their prayers.

By direction of the
Korean Commission
Syngman Rhee

To The President
and Mrs. Coolidge

Syngman Rhee *to* Grace Coolidge

Washington, D.C. • July 8, 1924

ON A WARM JUNE DAY IN 1924, 16-year-old Calvin Coolidge, Jr., and his older brother John played several games of tennis on the White House grounds. The younger boy didn't wear socks, and his exertions raised a blister on his foot. A few days later, Calvin Jr. was dead—felled by blood poisoning from the infected blister. ❧ The nation was shocked, and the White House was plunged into mourning. Earlier that month, buoyed by the "Coolidge prosperity" that boosted the nation's economy to new heights, the Republican Party's national convention had

named Coolidge its candidate in the 1924 presidential election. It should have been a happy time for Coolidge, but his grief was painfully obvious in the subdued tone of his campaign, and he later said that when his son died, "the power and the glory of the presidency went with him." The normally ebullient Grace Coolidge was similarly stricken, though she refused to allow her sorrow to interfere with her duties as First Lady.

Among the many messages of sympathy sent to the Coolidges that awful summer was this one from a man whose name was unfamiliar to most Americans: Syngman Rhee. In 1924, Korea was firmly under Japanese control, and Rhee was serving as president of the Korean provisional government in exile, based in Hawaii and Shanghai. No one doubted his convictions—because of his tireless advocacy of Korean independence, he had endured imprisonment and torture—but his authoritarian methods and contentious relations with other expatriate leaders made him a controversial figure.

Rhee's message to the Coolidges may have been a sincere gesture of kindness, but it almost certainly had another aim as well—to draw sympathetic attention to the cause of Korean independence. If so, it apparently failed, as indicated by a handwritten note in the corner of the letter: "Mr. MacMurray advises against acknowledging this." John Van Antwerp MacMurray headed the Division of Far Eastern Affairs at the U.S. State Department. His directive is a poignant reminder that life in the goldfish bowl of the White House sometimes means that even the deepest personal tragedy cannot override the niceties of international diplomacy and protocol.

Tragically, Americans were to become much better acquainted with Syngman Rhee in the following decades. After World War II, he became the first president of the newly independent South Korea. Then, without warning, troops from North Korea—joined later by Chinese forces—launched an invasion of the South in 1950, and the ensuing conflict cost more than 54,000 American lives. After the war, resentment of Rhee's autocratic regime sparked widespread unrest, and in 1960 he was back where he had been in 1924—in exile. ❧

EL COMODORO HOTEL
OPEN THE YEAR ROUND
250 ROOMS • 250 BATHS
T. R. KNIGHT, Proprietor. S. D. McCREARY, Manager

MIAMI, FLORIDA

June 18 - 1929

Mrs H. Hoover,
    Washington D.C.
You remember that Florida, Va
North Carolina Tenn & Texas
Gave Mr Hoover, a Large Majority
last fall Well "WE" Thought
we Were Putting a "real" White
"Lady" in the White House,
I didn't Even dream that you
would disgrace The White House
By Associating with Negroes

THE WOMEN'S LEAGUE OF MIAMI FLORIDA
to LOU HOOVER

Miami, Florida · June 18, 1929

A. E. BRUCE *to* LOU HOOVER

Claremont, California · June 16, 1929

O N JUNE 12, 1929, a group of congressmen's wives assembled for tea in the White House Red Room. First Lady Lou Hoover had hosted similar gatherings before, and this one shouldn't have rated more than a brief mention in the society pages of a few newspapers. This time, however, one of the guests, Mrs. Oscar DePriest, wife of the man who had been elected to the House of Representatives by the voters of the First Congressional District of Illinois, was black. ✖ It wasn't the first time that an African American had been a guest in the

Executive Mansion. Theodore Roosevelt had entertained educator Booker T. Washington at a White House dinner in 1901, and had been so roundly chastised for it that he never did such a thing again. His successors, fearing to offend their conservative political base, followed suit over the next three decades.

In 1929, at a time when lynchings were occurring with horrifying frequency across the South and soaring membership levels had turned the Ku Klux Klan into a genuinely powerful organization with a national following, the First Lady's well-intentioned gesture of hospitality struck a nerve and sparked a firestorm of criticism.

Predictably, many people expressed their feelings in letters to the White House. A few were primarily concerned about the

Jesse DePriest was the wife of the first African American to be elected to the U.S. Congress since Reconstruction.

political fallout from the First Lady's tea party: One man in Texas wrote, "I have much regret since Mr Hoover was our choice. Now the Jefferson Democrats are giving us Hoover Democrats the laugh." Most of the criticism, however, was firmly rooted in vicious, blatant, unapologetic racism. A woman in California voiced the fears of many: "If the bars are once thrown down the white race will soon disappear from the face of the earth." Another woman, this one in Florida, wrote, "It's very evident that you and Mr. Hoover are the results of the Yankee craze over the Black man and black gal during and prior to the Civil War. I knew it was in you both. . . ." A real estate agent in Omaha, Nebraska, sent a message whose tone of outrage was hardly surprising, coming as it did from a man whose neatly printed letterhead proudly proclaimed his refusal to sell or rent property to "Niggers, Japs or Chinks."

A few writers, on the other hand, were warmly supportive of Mrs. Hoover. The president of the "Colored Men's Regular Republican Ass'n Inc." in Jersey City, New Jersey, expressed his satisfaction in "knowing that you were too lofty of spirit, and too noble of character, and too Christian like in principal to do other wise than you did." And a man in Missouri assured her that she had shown "the true spirit of America" and that there were "millions of people . . . who believe you did absolutely right." He added, in a rueful postscript, "What a shame that, in this America we love, one should be called upon to apologize for being kind to a fellow human being."

The wildly divergent points of view expressed in the scores of messages sent to the White House in mid-June 1929 are encapsulated in these two letters, which were composed two days apart on opposite sides of the country.

The first is written in a furious scrawl by a nameless spokesperson for "The Women's League of Miami Fla" who is even more generous with her capitalization than she is with her underlining. Reminding the President's wife that southern voters played a major role in her husband's election, she says that the First Lady has betrayed those who "thought we were putting a 'real' White 'Lady' in the White House [and] didn't even dream that you would disgrace the White House by associating with Negroes." As far as the outraged members of the Women's League are concerned, the Hoovers can go to hell—or someplace even worse: "You can go to Illinois next winter and visit your Negro friends. FLORIDA Don't Care for you to visit the South any more."

The second is so warmly avuncular that it could have originated in Mister Rogers' Neighborhood. A. E. Bruce of California modestly introduces himself and his wife and presents their credentials: "Fortunately or unfortunately, we are 'white folks' but we have never been able to convince ourselves that the color of our skin had any particular relation to the size of our brains or the use to which we put them. . . ." Then he goes on to assure the First Lady of their support: "For the President and his wife we entertain the highest regard . . . and for them our prayers ascend."

It's exactly what Lou Hoover must have wanted, and needed, to hear. We can only hope that every embattled First Lady got a letter just like this one when she needed it most. ❧

June 16, 1929.

Mrs Herbert Hoover,

Washington, D. C.

Dear Mrs Hoover:-

      Mrs Bruce and I have been watching
with much interest the newspaper accounts of recent
occurrences at the White House.

      Fortunately or unfortunately, we are "white
folks" but we have never been able to convince
ourselves that the color of our skin had any particular relation to the size of our brains or the
use to which we put them; and we are quite sure, in
our own minds, that the non-discriminatory action
which you have recently taken, should merit only the
approval of all right minded people.

      For the President and his wife we entertain the
highest regard; with them, in the many problems
which arise constantly we sympathize; and for them our
prayers ascend, that they may be divinely guided in
leading our nation in all the paths of cultural and
spiritual progress.

      Respectfully,

        A. E. BRUCE.

A E Bruce

at School.

Dear Mrs. Hoover,
    We thank you for the nice fruit you sent. We thank you and the President for our school. Won't you visit us again? We like to have you come.
                    Your friend,
                    Evelyn Phillips.

at School..
        Dear Mrs Hoover.
    we thank you for
the fruit you sent
    we thank you and the president
        for our school.
won't your you visit us again.
    we liked to have you come.
            Your friend.
            myrtle weekley.

Students *to* Lou Hoover

Rapidan, Virginia · 1929

IN 1929, PRESIDENT AND MRS. HOOVER BOUGHT 164 acres of land on the eastern slope of the Blue Ridge Mountains, built a cluster of simply furnished rustic cabins, named the place Rapidan Camp, and used it as a much loved retreat where the President could escape what he called "the pneumatic hammer of public life." In a photograph from the period, Hoover stands in a stream, holding his fishing rod and wearing a jacket, stiff-collared white shirt, and necktie. ❧ On an early visit to the camp, the Hoovers learned that the children in the surrounding area had no school. This was

especially disturbing to the First Lady, who believed strongly in the importance of education. She must have been truly appalled by a 1929 report on conditions among families living only ten miles from Rapidan Camp. Most occupied two-room log cabins with dirt floors and a single

bed. The children were barefoot, ragged, and dirty ("Hygiene habits are few," the report noted tersely) and had no toys or books, though their parents did give them an occasional chew of tobacco.

To address the needs of their rural neighbors, the Hoovers established the President's Community School in 1930. A well-meaning Pennsylvania woman offered her services as "a special teacher of bobbin lace," but Mrs. Hoover's secretary informed her that becoming "more proficient in the rudiments of education" left the pupils (who reportedly ranged in age from six to twenty) no time in which to make lace.

These two notes are among several written to thank the First Lady for some "nice fruit" she had sent to the school. The words are identical, but the styles of handwriting are dramatically different— one painstakingly neat, the other practically illegible. The contrast hints at the challenges faced by the teacher in this tiny outpost of learning less than a hundred miles from the nation's capital. ❧

Lou Hoover meets with a teacher and her students in rural Madison County, Virginia, in 1930.

[Schmitt, P]

PHILIP SCHMITT

" Over Ten Years of Dependable Realty Service "

225 WEST PARK AVENUE
LONG BEACH, N. Y.

CORRESPONDENTS:
CANNES, FRANCE
LAKE PLACID, N. Y.

TELEPHONE
LONG BEACH 217
MAIL REPLY
POST OFFICE BOX 3
LONG BEACH, N. Y.

November 15,1932.

Mrs. Herbert Hoover,

My dear Mrs. Hoover,
May I call to your attention a very serious matter.Women every
where are practising what Americans call 'Hooverizing'.I do not
mean the destitute,but practically everyone.They are spurred on
by unimaginative executive secretaries following old lines suit
able for raising money for war-time or emergency where money is
raised in a normal community for immediate use in a distant place
  If only President Hoover before this Thanksgiving could lead the
American People in a prayer of thanks that in this year of bewild
erment the nations bins are full to bursting and that the women of
America are called upon,not,as in those other days,to deprive our
own families of sugar,butter,heat etc.that we could share with
strangers across the sea,but to provide generously for our own
and in the very act of putting that famous 'chicken'in our own
potsmake it possible for the farmer,the butcher,the delivery-
boy---perhaps even a cook and waitress to provide his or her fam
ily with the necessities of life.
  Things are unbelievably mixed up and rapidly becoming more so.
Allthrough the campaign I encounted angry and desperate store-
keepers literally cursing'Hooverizing'.
  The clipping I enclose of a campaign for an old time ' Hover'
Thanksgiving is the latest most organized sample of this really
dangerous idiocy.
  It is unbelievable but my sons economics professor said in
class that people had expected Hoover to break the depression
by declaring Heatless, Meatless,Wheatless days as he did during
the war.
  If only Mr.Hoover can change 'Hooverizing' into a rush to
buy the apples at our regular stores so that the man who should
be making the apple growers shoes need not sell apples on a stret
corner.You can do it I know.The woman who is holding onto a
teachers job besides a couple of others while mistress of our
State Executive Mansion couldnt understand.

Respectfully
Pearl N. Schmitt
(mrs. Philip Schmitt)

Goucher College '07.

Pearl N. Schmitt *to* Lou Hoover

Long Beach, New York • November 15, 1932

WHEN THIS LETTER WAS WRITTEN, the 1932 presidential election was over, and Lou Hoover knew that she was soon to be a *former* First Lady. Her husband had made a dismal showing in the election, carrying only six states and winning just 39 percent of the popular vote. The defeat was hardly surprising: Hoover had been swept into office on a tidal wave of unprecedented prosperity, but now those halcyon days were only a dim memory. The Great Depression had the nation by the throat. Banks were failing, unemployment was skyrocketing,

breadlines were lengthening, ruined businessmen were jumping out of windows, and housewives were worrying about how to get hold of the money to buy groceries and pay the rent and the gas bill.

Most people probably saw the bankers and brokers of Wall Street as the real villains of the tragic economic drama unfolding around them, but the President was widely blamed, too—first for having failed to rein the villains in, and then, as the crisis worsened, for failing to take decisive action to set things right. A firm subscriber to the philosophy of "rugged individualism," Hoover feared that massive programs of direct government aid would weaken the nation's moral fiber, a position that made him appear cold and unfeeling. He did eventually take some positive steps, such as approving a huge public-works program (Hoover Dam was its best known product) and establishing a government lending program to help farms and businesses, but he also stifled industrial production and exports by signing the highest peacetime tariff in

American history. The last straw came in the summer of 1932, when he summoned federal troops to disperse a ragtag "army" of veterans who marched on Washington to demand immediate payment of the bonus they had been promised. By then, the election was just months away, and Hoover's fate was sealed.

A family in Rapidan, Virginia, struggles with poverty and starvation during the Great Depression of the 1930s.

In an earlier stage of his public-service career, Hoover's laudable efforts to alleviate suffering in war-torn Europe and the flood-ravaged Mississippi Valley had led an admiring public to call him "The Great Humanitarian." But now, in an ironic twist that must have been deeply distressing to the Hoovers, men and women struggling to stay alive began to use the President's name as a bitter synonym for deprivation and misery: Hungry people referred to rabbits as "Hoover hogs," men seeking relief from the cold wrapped themselves in newspapers that they called "Hoover blankets," and homeless families built clusters of flimsy huts out of anything they could find and christened their grim shantytown "Hooverville."

This letter refers to another Hoover-inspired term that had originated some 15 years earlier. As U.S. food administrator during World War I, Hoover had initiated a voluntary program that urged Americans to conserve food through such measures as reducing waste, observing meatless Mondays and wheatless Wednesdays, and cutting back on the amount of sugar they added to their coffee and cornflakes. Officials called it "food conservation," and posters confidently proclaimed, "Food Will Win the War." Most people simply called it "Hooverizing." The ingenuity they employed in finding innovative ways to economize is hinted at in the editorial cartoon shown here, which appeared in the Kokomo [Indiana] Tribune. Notice the cook, frying pan in hand, eyeing the family cat as a possible source of protein. All jokes aside, Hooverizing was a rousing success: During the period when the policy was in effect, domestic food consumption dropped by 15 percent,

and the government was never forced to impose rationing.

Fast-forward to 1932. In a letter that fairly crackles with indignation, Pearl Schmitt (whose husband works in "realty services" and is probably having a hard time making a go of it) writes that while Hooverizing may have been a good thing in 1917, it most definitely is not called for now. She stoutly insists that even in "this year of bewilderment," there is plenty of food to go around ("the nations bins are full to bursting") and now that Thanksgiving is just around the corner, Americans should be consuming, not conserving. Recalling—without a hint of irony—Hoover's famous 1928 campaign promise of "a chicken in every pot," she tells the First Lady that the President should urge housewives to *spend, spend, spend*—not only to put food on their own families' tables but also to put some money in the pockets of people such as "the farmer, the butcher, the delivery-boy—perhaps even a cook and waitress," not to mention the street-corner apple-peddler "who should be making the apple growers shoes."

Alas, the situation was far more desperate than the shortsighted Mrs. Schmitt realized, and easy remedies were not to be found. American voters proved at the polls that they were ready for sweeping change, that they wanted a leader with energy and new ideas, and that they had had enough of Hoover. As the outgoing President and First Lady prepared to leave the White House for the last time, grim-faced men on the wintry streets of communities from coast to coast were turning their empty pockets inside out in a gesture of hopelessness they called "flying the Hoover flag." ❧

ARE YOU HOOVERIZING IN YOUR HOME?

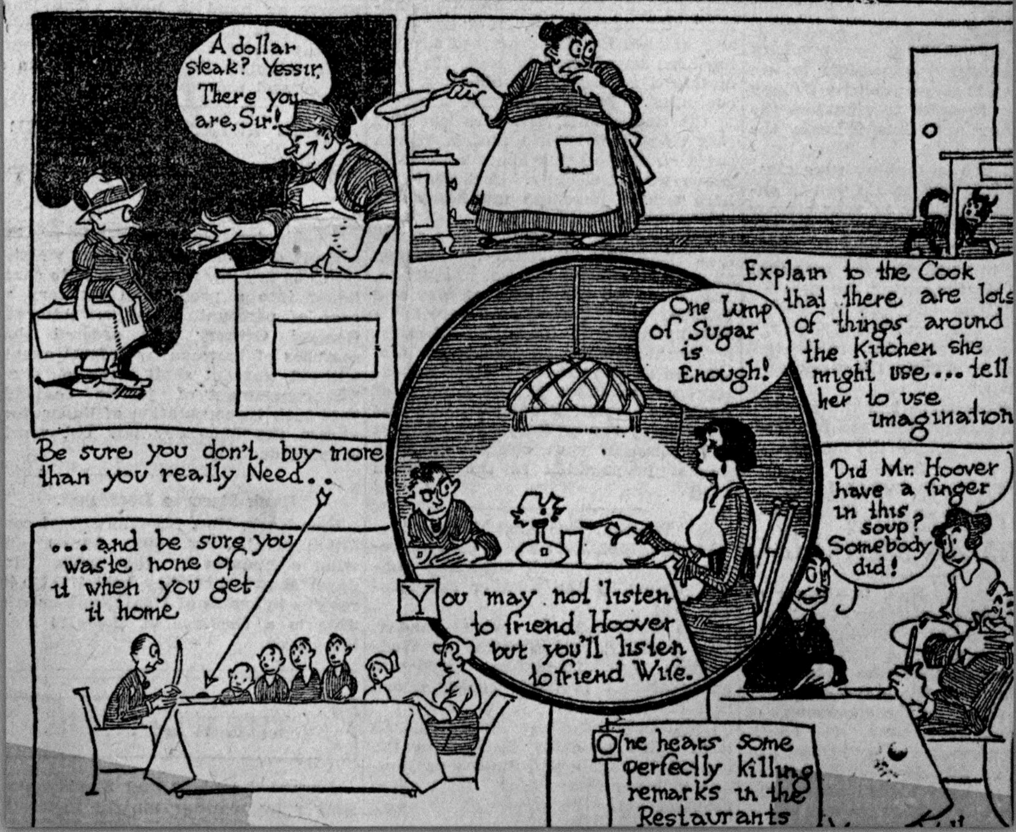

Up and down and around about

The house, you have gone with me.

In years gone by it has often been,

But in these days, constantly.

The house of beauty, the house of joy,

The house of sadness, of history.

Some ghosts are stately, and some grotesque

Some tragic, some gay, some humoresque.

Dear, - halls, and stairs and chambers wide

Still treasure the touch of your footstep light

And long for another glimpse of you.

January 23d, 1933

L.H.H.

Lou Hoover *to* Grace Coolidge

Washington, D.C. • January 23, 1933

FIRST LADIES PAST AND PRESENT ARE MEMBERS OF what may well be the world's most exclusive sorority. The experiences they have shared, not only the pageantry of motorcades and state dinners but also the challenge of maintaining a "normal" life and fighting to remain poised in the most trying circumstances, form a bond between them that transcends time and political party affiliation. ❧ Some First Ladies become mentors to their successors: Frances Cleveland, for example, frequently sought advice from Harriet Lane, who had lived in the White House decades before her.

Others simply become good friends, discovering shared interests and exchanging opinions about everything from international affairs to interior decoration.

Among the warmest of these relationships was the one that developed between Grace Coolidge and Lou Hoover. They had become friends when Hoover served as secretary of commerce in Coolidge's Cabinet, and they remained close for many years. In chatty letters, First Lady Lou told ex-First Lady Grace all about Rapidan Camp and reported on changes in the White House décor, and animal-lover Grace sent her friend a bird "which came over on the Zeppelin." They even coined nicknames for each other: "Lily of the Valley" for Lou, "Bleeding Heart" for Grace."

The warm tone of their correspondence is exemplified in a letter from January 1933 in which Mrs. Hoover invites Mrs. Coolidge to visit her one last time before the White House must be turned over to the incoming Roosevelts. Former President Coolidge had died less than three weeks earlier, and the First Lady knows that her friend might find comfort in a visit to the place where she and her late husband had spent happy, sad, and exciting times.

"My dear," she begins, "I am wondering whether any call of any kind tugs you this way? Is there any memory of anything that you would like to confirm? Any old haunts where you would like to pace alone? Any old memory you would like to relive?" She promises restful tranquility: "We could be very quiet—and see no one unless you wished. Or perhaps you want memories only, for a time."

Accompanying the letter is an 11-line poem that eloquently expresses what any First Lady must feel about the house that is at once an iconic shrine and a family home. "The house of beauty, the house of joy," she calls it, "The house of sadness, of history." Closing on a deeply personal note, she assures her friend and fellow member of the First Ladies sorority that ". . . halls, and stairs and chambers wide / Still treasure the touch of your footstep light / And long for another glimpse of you."

It's fitting that one of the world's great houses should be celebrated in one of the most gracious invitations ever written. ❧

Mar. 17th

33

Dearest Babs,

After a fruitless week of thinking and lying awake to find whether you need or want undies, dresses, hats, shoes, sheets, towels, rouge, soap plates, candy, flowers, lamps, laxative pills, whiskey, beer, etchings or caviar

I GIVE IT UP

!

And yet I know you lack some necessity of life — so go to it with my love & many happy returns of the day!

F.D.R.

FDR *to* Eleanor Roosevelt

Washington, D.C. • March 17, 1933

MILLIONS OF WORDS HAVE BEEN WRITTEN about the tangled and thorny relationship of Franklin and Eleanor Roosevelt, but much remains unknown and unknowable. ✻ When they married in 1905, he was handsome and self-confident, clearly a man on the way up; she was the shy, awkward product of a girlhood marred by her mother's aloofness and her father's alcoholism and death. Theirs was an unlikely union, but each saw something admirable and desirable in the other, and they forged a bond that lasted until Eleanor discovered that her husband had

been unfaithful to her. She thought about divorcing him, but there were five children to consider, and then Franklin was stricken with polio, so she stayed. The intimate side of her marriage was destroyed, but her respect for her husband's strength and intellect did not falter.

By the time this note was written, in March of 1933, the Roosevelts were just settling into the roles they were to play for the remainder of their lives together: He was to be the inspiring leader, guiding the nation through crisis after crisis, while she would serve as his eyes and ears and legs and conscience, all while throwing herself into a variety of worthy and sometimes unpopular causes.

FDR's note jokingly depicts a husband's befuddlement over what to give his wife for their wedding anniversary. Employing the irrepressibly jaunty tone that endeared him to millions of people, he lists several possible gifts, from lingerie and beer to soup plates and laxative pills, before throwing up his hands ("I GIVE IT UP!") and telling her to

pick out something for herself. The letter is not very romantic, especially when we compare it with the Grants' 1875 anniversary notes to each other—but then this First Lady didn't expect much from her husband in the way of romance, and she was far too busy to worry about presents. ✻

Newlyweds Franklin and Eleanor Roosevelt are caught in a candid moment in Newburgh, New York, on May 7, 1905.

My room —
for Two Dollars! And I suspect
bed bugs!

[LH to ER]

Tuesday,
November 28th

[1933]

Madame!

Now will you please tell
me what in the world one
is going to do about cases
like these?

I just came in from along
trek with the chairman of the
county relief committee. He
put them up to me — and
I pass them on to you,
not expecting or asking you
for anything except ideas. But

LORENA HICKOK *to* ELEANOR ROOSEVELT

Charles City, Iowa • November 28, 1933

URING THEIR LIFETIME, Eleanor Roosevelt and Lorena Hickok were usually described as "good friends," but a cache of letters opened to public view in 1978 revealed what the *Washington Post* described as "clear indications of lesbianism" and fueled speculation that the two women had been lovers. Still, as one biographer has noted, "We can never know what people do in the privacy of their own rooms. The door is closed. The blinds are drawn. We don't know." ❦ Lorena Hickok was a highly regarded Associated Press reporter (and the first woman to have a byline on the front page of the *New York Times*) who was assigned to cover Mrs. Roosevelt during the 1932 presidential campaign. Despite the differences in their backgrounds—one had grown up in the precincts of privilege, the other had known poverty and physical abuse—the unlikely pair soon discovered that they had much in common and greatly enjoyed each other's company. By Christmastime they had grown so close that Lorena gave Eleanor a sapphire and diamond ring.

Soon after the Roosevelts moved into the White House, the women realized that their relationship was compromising Lorena's objectivity as a reporter. Leaving the Associated Press and the career that had meant so much to her, "Hick" went to work as an investigator for the Federal Emergency Relief Agency (FERA), crisscrossing the country to assess the effectiveness of the New Deal programs that had been developed to help people survive the Depression.

In addition to providing detailed reports to her bosses at FERA, Lorena described her findings to the First Lady in letters such as this one from 1933. Written on hotel stationery, with a picture on which Lorena has indicated the location of her two-dollar room and its "suspected" bedbugs, it describes the plight of two Iowa families.

Refusing to apply for county relief, one man and his wife have managed to survive for more than two years on just $126, but now they may have to give up their home in order to pay their taxes. Another elderly couple has worked hard and sacrificed to send their son to college, where he gets by on a dollar a week and may well "break himself down" from overwork. Lorena's question, which is repeated several times in her 12-page letter, is heartfelt: "What can be done?"

These firsthand reports not only played a key role in improving government relief programs but also inspired the First Lady to become personally involved in finding ways to help people get through the hard times. The job kept "Hick" on the road a great deal, but whenever she was in Washington, she slept in a White House bedroom next to Eleanor's. ❦

2134 N.W. 1st Ct.
Miami, Fla.
Dec. 14, 1934.

Mrs. Franklin D. Roosevelt.
Washington, D.C.
Dear Madam —.

I am a widow
with a son fourteen
years of age and am
trying to support him
and myself and keep
him in school on a
very small sum which
I make.

I feel worthy of
asking you about this:
I am greatly in need
of a coat. If you have
one which you have
laid aside from last
season would appreciate

CLARA LEONARD *to* ELEANOR ROOSEVELT

Miami, Florida • December 14, 1934

I N DECEMBER 1934, the temperature in South Florida sank to levels that were most decidedly nontropical. In fact, according to the federal government's Natural Resources Conservation Service, that month saw the coldest temperature—26 degrees—ever recorded in Miami. ❧ Little wonder that Clara Leonard needed a coat. Presumably, she first sought help from local relief agencies, but in a place like Miami, they probably didn't have a big stock of coats at their disposal. Perhaps feeling that she had nowhere else to turn, Mrs. Leonard wrote this letter to the President's wife. The fact that she did so speaks volumes about how Eleanor Roosevelt was perceived by the people who were hit hardest by the Depression: She was accessible, a down-to-earth person who genuinely cared about

the problems of the "little people." She would help if she could.

Judging by the tone of her letter, Mrs. Leonard is embarrassed to have to ask for help, but nonetheless she feels "worthy" of it. She is a widow with a teenage son, she is working but still has very little money, and it's cold outside. She doesn't want anything fancy, or even brand-new; a coat that Mrs. Roosevelt might have "laid aside from last season" will do fine. She even offers to pay the postage.

We don't know whether the First Lady actually saw this letter; even if she did, it's possible that she didn't have a coat—even last year's model—to give away. In any case, a White House secretary sent a pro forma response to Mrs. Leonard, assuring her that Mrs. Roosevelt "would like to assist all those who appeal to her" but has found it impossible to attempt to comply with "the great number of similar requests she receives."

We can only hope that it soon got warmer in Miami and that Clara Leonard got by. ❧

A photograph from the 1930s Federal Art Project highlights the yawning gap between poverty and affluence.

Brooklyn N. Y.
5/8-35.

Ack'd
5/17/35

Dear Mrs. Roosevelt.

Over a year ago, I discovered an ingredient of vegetable extraction, which removes dandruff.

I have demonstrated my method before several eminent persons, who are interested in hair and scalp research, but who seem to resent the fact that I, not a medical student, possess that marvelous formula.

Doctors tell me that eight out of ten people have dandruff, it is an unsanitary condition of the scalp, of years of accumulation, that nothing has as yet has been able to combat.

Realizing how badly in need of this eliminature thousands of people are, I find it difficult to make the proper contact.

Knowing of your great interest, in the betterment of all things, I have taken this privilege of writing you, for whatever advice or guidance, you can give me.

MRS. H. GOLDFARB *to* ELEANOR ROOSEVELT

Brooklyn, New York • May 8, 1935

IN 1935, THE WHOLE WORLD SEEMED TO BE SLIDING INTO CHAOS. Under the leadership of the increasingly bellicose Adolf Hitler, Germany announced the creation of a new air force, reinstated compulsory military service, reasserted control over the Saar region, and stripped Jews of many of their rights as citizens. Beloved humorist Will Rogers died in a plane crash, and Senator Huey Long was assassinated in the Louisiana state capitol he had built. In an attempt to build an empire like that of ancient Rome, Mussolini invaded Ethiopia; on the other side of the globe, Japanese troops occupied a demilitarized zone in China. Growing tension between Republicans and Nationalists in Spain hinted that civil war was imminent. A powerful hurricane ravaged the Florida Keys, an earthquake killed 40,000 people in what is now Pakistan, and on an April day that came to be known as Black Sunday, a dust storm darkened the sky over American cities from Oklahoma to the Atlantic Ocean.

In the midst of all this gloomy news, there were a few bright spots. The relentlessly charming seven-year-old Shirley Temple became the youngest person to win an Academy Award. Amelia Earhart made the first solo flight from Hawaii to California. Julie Andrews and Elvis Presley were born. At a track meet in Michigan, Jesse Owens broke five world records in a single afternoon. And in Brooklyn, New York, a woman named Goldfarb had a surefire cure for dandruff.

At first glance, Mrs. Goldfarb's letter to Eleanor Roosevelt appears to be a request for a high-profile endorsement of her "wonderful achievement." Such a request wouldn't be unusual. In 1927, Mrs. Roosevelt (described as a woman "whose wide interests reflect her generous, many-sided personality") appeared in a full-page ad for Simmons mattresses in *Pictorial Review* magazine, and scores of other prominent women—including some First Ladies—have allowed their names and faces to appear in ads touting a variety of goods and services.

In this instance, however, Mrs. Goldfarb only wants advice on getting her product on the market. She knows that dandruff is an "unhealthy and unsanitary condition which exists among all people," and she knows her "ingredient of vegetable extraction" is effective in eliminating it, having demonstrated that fact "before several eminent persons, who are interested in hair and scalp research." Tragically, she has run afoul of the green-eyed monster of jealousy: Those in a position to help her "seem to resent the fact that I, not a medical student, possess that marvelous formula."

We know that Eleanor Roosevelt was generally unconcerned about her appearance, but there's no evidence to suggest she had dandruff. In any case, she didn't weigh in on Mrs. Goldfarb's behalf. Instead, the First Lady's secretary sent the frustrated inventor a brief note suggesting that she contact the Department of Commerce. ✤

February 26, 1939.

My dear Mrs. ~~Robert~~ Jr. *Henry M.*

I am afraid that I have never been a very
useful member of the Daughters of the
American Revolution, so I know it will
make very little difference to you whether
I resign, or whether I continue to be a
member of your organization.

However, I am in complete disagreement
with the attitude taken in refusing
Constitution Hall to a great artist.
You have set an example which seems to
me unfortunate, and I feel obliged to
send in to you my resignation.   You
had an opportunity to lead in an enlightened way and it seems to me that your
organization has failed.

I realize that many people will not agree
with me, but feeling as I do this seems
to me the only proper procedure to
follow.

        Very sincerely yours,

ELEANOR ROOSEVELT *to* MRS. HENRY M. ROBERT, JR.

Washington, D.C. · February 26, 1939

I N THE 1930S, FAMED AFRICAN-AMERICAN CONTRALTO Marian Anderson was greeted by cheering audiences at opera houses and concert halls all over Europe. But it was a different story when her manager tried to arrange a concert in Washington, D.C., in 1939: The city's only suitable auditorium was Constitution Hall, owned by the Daughters of the American Revolution—and the DAR refused to open the hall to a black performer. ❧ Among those offended by the organization's stand was First Lady Eleanor Roosevelt, who was both a passionate champion of equal rights and a DAR member. Doubtless aware that her action would upset many of her husband's supporters, especially in the South, she wasted no time in sending this letter of resignation to the DAR's president general. The letter is brief, but it leaves no doubt about the First Lady's feelings: "You had an opportunity to lead in an enlightened way and it seems to me that your organization has failed."

In her response, Mrs. Robert regretted that she had not been in Washington when the furor erupted. "Perhaps I might have been able to remove some of the misunderstanding and to have presented to you personally the attitude of the Society," she wrote. But the damage was done.

In the end, the DAR's intransigence sparked an event that became a landmark in civil rights history: Secretary of the Interior Harold Ickes arranged for Marian Anderson to sing on the steps of the Lincoln Memorial on Easter Sunday, 1939. The electrifying performance drew some 75,000 people—the largest crowd assembled on the Mall up to that time—and a radio audience of millions.

A few months later, Anderson received the NAACP's Spingarn Medal; the award was presented by Eleanor Roosevelt. And in 1943, as part of a benefit for the American Red Cross, Marian Anderson sang at Constitution Hall. ❧

Eleanor Roosevelt presents an award to singer Marian Anderson in Richmond, Virginia, July 3, 1939.

May 22, 1942.

Mrs. Eleanor Roosevelt,
The White House,
Washington, D.C.

My dear Mrs. Roosevelt:

I am writing to you as one American woman to
another about the plight of the Japanese-
Americans in the western part of our country.
I do not doubt that you are receiving, as I
am, many letters from Americans, not Japanese,
protesting against the inhuman and cruel treatment of the Japanese-Americans. It is not only
what is being done to the Japanese but it is the
effect upon our own people that is so evil.

I want to do anything I can but I write to ask
your advice as to what can be done. It seems to
me that the way that these people are being
treated is so much more German than it is American.

I enclose copies of some of the letters which I
have received within the last few days.

Very sincerely yours,

Pearl S. Buck

PSB HS
Encs.

I understand military necessity, but not the way in which it is being done.

PSB.

PEARL S. BUCK *to* ELEANOR ROOSEVELT

Perkasie, Pennsylvania • May 22, 1942

WHEN PRESIDENT ROOSEVELT SIGNED EXECUTIVE ORDER 9066 in February 1942, the civil rights of thousands of people were not only violated but obliterated. The order authorized the Army to designate "military areas" from which "any or all persons may be excluded." In response, more than 110,000 Japanese Americans—most of them citizens of this country—were uprooted from their homes and confined in war relocation camps because their presence on the West Coast supposedly constituted a threat to the security of a nation at war with Japan. &

The relocation was in full swing when Eleanor Roosevelt received this letter from author Pearl Buck, winner of both the Pulitzer Prize and the Nobel Prize in literature, who had devoted her life to building bridges between East and West. Writing "as one American woman to another," Buck

protests the "inhuman and cruel treatment" of the evacuees—but she expresses particular concern about the internment's impact on the nation's soul. She insists that "it is the effect upon our own people that is so evil," adding, "the way these people are being treated is so much more German than it is American."

Scrawled across the letter is the First Lady's response, which was typed and sent to Buck a few days later. "I regret the need to relocate," she says, "but I recognize it has to be done." Having heard "high praise" for the Army's handling of the complicated process, she says, with a figurative shrug of her shoulders, that the resettlement "is being as well done as could be expected."

It is, of course, a cop-out. Internment was bitterly unfair, morally wrong, utterly unnecessary, and, as the Supreme Court eventually affirmed, unconstitutional. The First Lady's failure to recognize this is all the more disappointing because it betrays her passionate commitment to the protection of human rights. This time she got it wrong. &

Members of the Mochida family await evacuation during the Japanese internment ordered by President Roosevelt.

Joe Louis once said "we are
on God's side. yes it might
be true, but God never captains
a jim crow army, now does he
reach down and give Negro
soldier's a drink of water in
a paper cup.
        Mrs I'm going to fight,

here. I was served yes in a
paper cup, while a white man
beside me was served in a glass.
Asking why the paper cup, I was
told it was the policy of the state.
        Please note, I'm expected
to be call to active service very
soon, I have a lot to fight for
so the white man says. My four
brothers are in the service, but

I realize you are for the common
man, and your husband also
but for the other people (whites)
Hitler & the japs could win
the war if it meant giving the
Negro equality.

        On
the radio
japs, "
yellow
I'm ne
you hu
Soldier
seo is

Pvt. Clifton Searles
E.R.C. Unassigned U.S. Army
13,178,798
C/o Lincoln University
Lincoln University Pa
Box B09
Jan 11th 1942
            8:25.

Mrs. Roosevelt:
        While visiting your
        the headquarters of the
        I had a most interesting
        happen.
        I stopped at the People's
        me, 7th & M. Street N.W. and
        a small soda. The clerk
        another clerk, one coke
        . My instance reply
        don't want to take. it
        should like to drink it

P.S.
here is the cups, to bad
some Negro boy couldn't
give a dying boy (white)
a cooling drink on a
battle field. God bless the
white man, and teach him
something about brotherhood
& Democracy.

PVT. CLIFTON SEARLES *to* ELEANOR ROOSEVELT

Lincoln University, Pennsylvania • January 11, 1943

ELEANOR ROOSEVELT *to* PVT. CLIFTON SEARLES

Washington, D.C. • January 23, 1943

A T FIRST GLANCE, IT'S HARD TO TELL EXACTLY WHAT THE THING IS. Only gradually do you realize that it's a paper drinking cup, squashed flat, with some writing on it. It looks like a piece of trash—not exactly the kind of thing you'd expect to find in an envelope in the White House mail room. But you assume it must be important somehow, because somebody took the trouble to send it to Eleanor Roosevelt. ❧ Your assumption is correct. It *is* important, not because it possesses any intrinsic value (it is just what it seems, a perfectly ordinary Dixie cup),

but because it symbolizes an injustice that hasn't yet been fully made right.

Clifton Searles was a private in the U.S. Army, visiting Washington, D.C., "the headquarters of the nation." He was young and black, and on the 11th of January 1943, he was thirsty. He went into a drugstore and asked for a Coke, which was served to him in a paper cup, although the other customers—the white customers, that is—were drinking their sodas from proper glasses. When he asked why, the man behind the counter told him it was "the policy of the store."

It's the kind of racial discrimination that black Americans had to contend with every day, but Private Searles's letter makes it clear that this time it really stings. As he stands there at the drugstore counter in his Army uniform, expecting to be called to active duty any day, he reflects bitterly on the fact that he has four brothers in

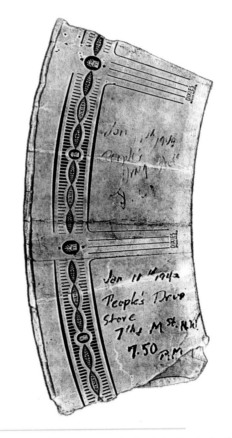

Pvt. Clifton Searles crushed and sent this paper cup with his letter as tangible evidence of the discrimination he faced.

Already compelling, the letter gains immediacy and enormous power from four words Private Searles adds to the postscript: "Here is the cup."

He knows that a thing becomes undeniably real only when you can touch it. He sends the cup to the White House for the same reason that he carried it out of that drugstore: Even though it's flattened and fragile, the cup is a heavy reminder of the soul-wounding bigotry that a black soldier can run into in the most unlikely places, and he wants the First Lady to feel the weight of it.

Of course Mrs. Roosevelt, for all her good intentions, couldn't wipe away the racial inequality that affected millions of men and women like Private Searles. So she did what she could, sending him a 15-line response in an attempt to make him feel better. "I can quite understand how what happened to you made you feel as bitterly as you do feel," she writes, adding something Private Searles already knows: American society tolerates too many "things of that kind." Invoking the enemies against whom the young soldier may soon be fighting, she reminds him that "under the Germans or the Japanese you would have very little freedom, and you certainly would not have the freedom to write to me as you have." She closes with the glib assurance that "a larger and larger group of white people . . . are conscious of the wrongs and . . . are helping to correct them."

The words must have sounded hollow to Mrs. Roosevelt even as she wrote them. The crushed paper cup lay on the desk in front of her, a reminder and a rebuke. ✺

the service, "but as to what they are fighting for God only knows," adding wryly, "I'm going to feel fine, fighting in a Jim Crow army, for a Jim Crow government." He remembers having heard famed boxer Joe Louis assert that America was fighting on God's side, but now Private Searles can't help thinking bitterly that God "never captains a jim crow army, nor does he reach down and give Negro soldier's a drink of water in a paper cup." The more he thinks about the whole ugly incident, the angrier he gets—so angry that you can imagine him furiously clenching the muscles in his jaw as he allows himself to consider the possibility of revenge: "Yes I'm going to fight, but I'll be fighting for my race, for my people, and when I might see a white boy dying on a battle field, I hope to God I won't remember People's Drug Store on January 11th."

Pvt. Clifton Searles signed this photograph of himself as "just another soldier."

January 23, 1943.

Dear Mr. Searles:

  I can quite understand how
what happened to you made you feel as
bitterly as you do feel. There are many
things of that kind which many of us in
this country deeply regret. The only
thing I can say to you is that under the
Germans or the Japanese you would have
very little freedom, and you certainly
would not have the freedom to write to me
as you have. You are free to go on working as a people for the betterment of
your people and you are gradually gathering behind you a larger and larger group
of white people who are conscious of the
wrongs and who are helping to correct them.

  Very sincerely yours,

Private Clifton Searles
E.R.C. Unassigned
c/o Lincoln University
Box 209
Lincoln University, Pennsylvania.   VDS

Memphis, Tenn. June 23, 1943
Dear Mrs. R -
        Well, John L Lewis declares
another "truce" until October 31. Seems he
does as he pleases. Maybe he has had a
"truce" declared on that Anti-Strike Bill.
Why dont FDR sign it?
        That race riot in Detroit is a
terrible and horrible thing. Race friction
all over our country ,due largely, we believe,
to your unwise talks and actions. Why dont
you stay home and quit talking and writing
on every thing under the sun? you and others
should forget that 4 and 5th terms and get
busy on the WAR and food for the USA. Willkie
or Dewey 'll do.   Jeff Davis

Nash. June 24, 1943.
Dear Madam:
    The blood of the dead
in Detroit is on
your head — And you
cannot deny it.
        Yours truly,
        Frances Jackson

Lorena Hickok *to* Eleanor Roosevelt

Long Island, New York · April 13, 1945

I
N THE SPRING OF 1945, weary Americans had reason to believe that the long war against Nazi Germany would soon be over. Then, on April 12, Franklin Roosevelt— the only President many people had ever known—died of a cerebral hemorrhage. ❧ By then, relations between Eleanor Roosevelt and Lorena Hickok had cooled. Eleanor's hectic schedule made it difficult for the two to spend much time together, and Lorena became increasingly angry about the press's coverage of her as the First Lady's "first friend." By late 1934, their correspondence, though still affectionate, was marked by occasional flashes of

anger and frequent apologies for hurt feelings. Eleanor revealed her state of mind in a 1935 letter: "What a nuisance hearts are. . . ." Early in 1945, Lorena left Washington and settled on Long Island. She was there when she learned of FDR's death and promptly sent this letter to Eleanor.

Her first words express what most Americans were thinking: I can't believe he's gone. She recalls Roosevelt's having been "so strong, so vital, so full of energy" and notes that "one never had to worry about the President letting anybody run him"—something she isn't ready to say about Harry Truman. Then she speaks directly to the woman she still loves. "For you and your future I have no worries at all," she tells Eleanor. "You will find your place—a very active and important place, I feel sure—and fill it superbly." ❧

The casket of Franklin Roosevelt moves toward its final resting place in Hyde Park on April 14, 1945.

Harry Truman *to* Bess Truman

Washington, D.C. • *June 12, 1945*

BESS TRUMAN, WHO DIDN'T CARE MUCH for what she once called "this awful public life," defined her role this way: "A woman's place in public is to sit beside her husband, be silent, and be sure her hat is on straight." In seven years as First Lady, she never held a press conference or sat for a proper interview. ❦ At one point she agreed to answer a list of questions submitted by reporters, but her responses were hardly revealing: "*Q: Has living in the White House changed your views on politics and people? A: No comment.*" When she was asked, "Mrs. Truman,

how will we ever get to know you?" she snapped, "You don't need to know me. I'm only the President's wife and the mother of his daughter." It was the only job she knew how to do, and it was all her husband asked of her.

A widely repeated story says that Truman once found his wife burning a batch of their letters. When he protested, "Bess, think of history!" she replied, "I am." If true, the anecdote should make us especially grateful that this warm and deeply personal letter, written two months after he took office, escaped the flames.

Truman had told reporters that the news of Franklin Roosevelt's sudden death made him feel "like the moon, the stars and all the planets had fallen on me." Some of that initial shock and bewilderment is still evident in this letter, which begins with a wistful recollection of the way life used to be: "Just two months ago today, I was a reasonably happy and contented Vice-President. . . . But things have changed so much it hardly seems real." Now, trying to get some work done in the White House study, he is distracted by creaking floors and rustling drapes that "move back and

forth." The ghosts of former Presidents "walk up and down the hall," he reports, but they don't scare him. Instead, he eavesdrops on their conversations ("I can just imagine old Andy and Teddy having an argument over Franklin") and shares his less-than-flattering opinion of his predecessors ("Or James Buchanan and Franklin Pierce deciding which was the more useless to the country"). He chats about what he's been doing, hopes she's having a good time, and closes with the hope that she'll write to him every day. The underlying theme couldn't be simpler: His wife is out of town and he misses her, because he depends on her.

Being President changes a man. He needs lots of people to help him do the job well, but he also needs someone to remind him who he used to be, to help him maintain a connection with the man the people elected. By all accounts, that's what Bess Truman did for her husband— and, by all accounts, he thanked God for her every day. If he didn't, he should have. By reminding him who he was, she helped him become the kind of President the country, and the times, needed. ❦

Elizabeth Arden

691 FIFTH AVENUE · NEW YORK

Dear Mrs. Eisenhower:

Thank you so much for the nice compliments on my Washington salon! I am delighted that you find both staff and service to your liking. We promise always to do our best, for it is our pleasure to grant your every wish whenever possible.

When you first returned from Paris I thought your hair looked really beautiful, but it did not seem quite the same in subsequent newspaper photographs...so I suggested that Gladys have Stanislaus draw a structural diagram, with complete instructions.

The sketch has just arrived, and I am asking the young woman who does your hair to study it very carefully...and practice, practice, practice!...until she has your special hair-do down perfectly! When you come into the salon again I hope you will find the results especially pleasing. I am inclosing a diagram for your personal use, thinking it might be helpful during your travels.

With all my best wishes,

Most sincerely

Elizabeth Arden

February twentieth, 1953

ELIZABETH ARDEN *to* MAMIE EISENHOWER

New York, New York • February 20, 1953

MAMIE EISENHOWER'S VIEW OF HER ROLE AS THE WIFE of a public figure was encapsulated in a headline that appeared in 1955: "Mamie Eisenhower: First Lady—But Wife First." While that view of a woman's "place" is out of favor today, millions of women in the 1950s wanted to be just like Mamie, and millions of men dreamed of finding a wife like her waiting at the front door, wearing a pretty dress and proffering a martini. ❧ When Dwight Eisenhower became president of Columbia University in 1948 and later was named commander of NATO forces, Mamie

perfected the art of being a supremely gracious hostess. She also established a reputation as something of a clothes-horse, inspiring a fashion columnist to gush in 1952, ". . . finally we shall have a woman in the White House who is fashion-aware." She favored styles that were feminine and youthful (she once said that she hated "old-lady clothes") and was especially fond of pink; her rhinestone-sprinkled Inaugural Ball gown attracted so much attention that its color was soon dubbed "First Lady Pink."

People seemed particularly fascinated by Mamie's hairstyle, especially the bangs that became her trademark. An anony-mous writer once advised Mamie that she "would look much nicer if you didn't wear your hair like a six-year-old kid," but instead of redoing her hairdo, the First Lady got some high-level advice on how to perfect it.

In this letter, which was written just a month after Ike's first Inauguration, beauty magnate Elizabeth Arden promises the new President's wife that the stylist

in her Washington salon will "practice, practice, practice! . . . until she has your special hair-do down perfectly!" She even provides a set of nine sketches—the final one is seen here, featuring a model who doesn't look much like Mamie—that will enable any hairdresser to cut, curl, and comb the First Lady's signature coiffure. The bangs stayed. ❧

This hand-drawn sketch is one of nine that Elizabeth Arden sent to Mamie Eisenhower in 1953.

1953 JUN 16 PM 2 05

WA1525 LONG NL PD

NEW YORK NY JUNE 15

MRS DWIGHT D EISENHOWER

THE WHITE HOUSE

I TURN TO YOU IN MY DEEP GRIEF AND IMPLORE YOU TO

INTERCEDE WITH PRESIDENT EISENHOWER TO GRANT MERCY TO

MY BELOVED CHILDREN. I BEG OF YOU TO ACT THROUGH

THE CHARITY OF YOUR HEART FOR AN OLD WOMAN WHOSE DAYS

ARE SPENT IN WEEPING. I BEG OF YOU TO THINK OF TWO

CHILDREN FOR WHOM HIS HOLINESS POPE PIUS HAS EXPRESSED

COMPASSION IN HIS APPEAL FOR MERCY. I WILL PRAY

TO THE GOD OF ALL OF US FOR YOU IN THANKFULNESS FOR

YOUR COMPASSIONATE HELP

MRS SOPHIE ROSENBERG   36 LAUREL HILL TERRACE

NEW YORK CITY.

SOPHIE ROSENBERG *to* MAMIE EISENHOWER

New York, New York • June 15, 1953

AS THE 1950S BEGAN, a series of hammer blows left Americans deeply worried. Behind the new and menacing Iron Curtain, the Soviet Union detonated its own atomic bomb. Spies were unmasked in high-level positions, and Senator Joseph McCarthy claimed to have proof that the government was riddled with them. ❧ As the anti-Communist paranoia mounted, Julius and Ethel Rosenberg were arrested and charged with passing atomic secrets to the Russians. They insisted they were innocent, and the evidence against Ethel was somewhat flimsy—but after a trial that drew

worldwide media attention, they were convicted and sentenced to death.

As the appeals dragged on for two years, the White House was deluged with letters. One of them was from Ethel Rosenberg, who begged President Eisenhower to stop "the savage destruction of a small unoffending Jewish family." "Take counsel with the mother of your only son," she wrote;

"her heart must plead my cause with grace and with felicity!"

Ethel wasn't alone in thinking that Mamie Eisenhower might be a sympathetic ally: Just four days before the scheduled execution date, Julius Rosenberg's mother sent this impassioned telegram to the First Lady herself. But the President was convinced of the Rosenbergs' guilt, and Mrs. Eisenhower, who took her role as supportive spouse very seriously, apparently made no attempt to change his mind.

Still maintaining their innocence, the Rosenbergs went to the electric chair on June 19, 1953. They were the only two American civilians executed for espionage during the Cold War, and Ethel was the first woman executed by the federal government since Mary Surratt was hanged in 1865 for her role in the Lincoln assassination conspiracy.

Since the end of the Cold War, new evidence—including a passage in Nikita Khrushchev's memoirs—confirms the fact that Julius Rosenberg was engaged in espionage. The extent of Ethel's involvement is still unclear. ❧

At a rally in New York City, Sophie Rosenberg appeals to President Eisenhower on June 11, 1953, to save her son, Julius.

Julie and Patricia Nixon *to* Mamie Eisenhower

Washington, D.C. • November 17, 1954

THE LIVES OF TRICIA AND JULIE NIXON exemplify the highs and lows of life in the glitzy goldfish bowl that is the White House. The girls never knew a life outside of politics, following their father as he moved up the ladder from the House of Representatives to the Vice President's office, stirring controversy and drama at every step. They didn't make it to the White House in 1960—more drama— but they triumphantly moved in eight years later. ❧ Jerry and Betty Ford's daughter, Susan, once gleefully described how much she enjoyed holding her senior prom in the

East Room and sneaking into the White House kitchen to fill her pockets from the huge stock of cookies always kept there.

The Nixon girls were a bit too old for that kind of fun, but they had their White House moments nonetheless. Julie took an active interest in foreign policy, occasionally filled in for her mother at events, and joined two famous presidential names by marrying David Eisenhower, grandson of Dwight. Tricia accompanied her father on some of his state visits and was the radiant centerpiece of a fairy-tale Rose Garden wedding in 1971.

Both sisters eventually found themselves defending their parents. Julie's outspokenness during the Watergate crisis led one journalist to call her the President's "First Lady in practice if not in fact," and she later wrote a loving and well-received biography of her mother. Even Tricia, who rarely spoke in public, broke her habitual silence to deny a biographer's claim that President Nixon had struck his wife. "My mother was not a fragile flower," Tricia insisted. "She would have left forever if anything like that had happened."

All of that—the excitement, the fun, the glamour, the heartbreak—was far in the future and utterly unimaginable in November 1954. Tricia was eight and Julie was six when their mother persuaded them to get out their crayons and draw pictures for First Lady Mamie Eisenhower's birthday. Julie's is pretty straightforward, a big cake with towering candles and patriotic icing. Tricia's is a bit more ambitious—she was older, after all, and perhaps a bit more adept with scissors—with little cutout windows like an Advent calendar.

The First Lady declared that she was delighted with the girls' artwork. "You used wonderful colors," she wrote to Julie, "and I surely do thank you for it." Her note to Tricia said, "I just loved the little windows . . . and peeked through each one and found a surprise every time." Mamie, who had grandchildren about the same age as the Nixon kids, had obviously been on the receiving end of this kind of gift many times before.

Is that tape on the top edge of Patricia's picture? Dare we hope that someone mounted it on the door of the White House refrigerator? ❧

1

301 Union Avenue
Peekskill, N.Y.
Feb. 19, 1862

Dear Mrs. Kennedy,

Recently I read in the newspaper that you were going on a tour to India from March 2 to March 25. You see I have a pen-pal in India and I was wondering if it would be at all possible for me to accompany you on your trip. My pen-pal's name is Veena Mahajan and she lives in New Delhi. This for me would be the most important thing in my whole life.

I realize you are very busy and get many letters but even if this letter only gets to your

2

MICHELE TIMMONS *to* JACQUELINE KENNEDY

Peekskill, New York · *February 19, 1962*

I
T'S NEVER FUN TO BE LEFT BEHIND, especially when you miss a once-in-a-lifetime experience. ❧ When Michele Timmons heard that Jackie Kennedy was going to India, she used her best teenage-girl stationery to send a letter to the White House. "I have a pen-pal in India," she writes, "and I was wondering if it would be at all possible for me to accompany you." After insisting that the trip "would be the most important thing in my whole life," she decides that a little sweet talk might help: "I think you are the prettiest First Lady the U.S. ever had." Sadly, even a page full of "Oh please

oh please oh pretty please" wouldn't have made any difference. Mrs. Kennedy's secretary wrote, "We are sorry that your letter reached us too late . . . and your request cannot be granted."

Even though Michele didn't get to go along, the First Lady's visit to India was a triumph. She called on President Rajendra Prasad; laid a bouquet at the site of Mohandas Gandhi's cremation; visited a hospital and a home for vagrant boys; and played the part of a tourist with a boat ride on the Ganges, a visit to the Taj Mahal, and a brief ride on the back of an elephant. The press covered every moment of it, documenting the details of her wardrobe and wrestling with phrases like "apricot silk ziberline" and "scarlet, orange and hot pink printed and ribbed silk matelasse by Gustave Tassell."

Although she always insisted that she had no desire for celebrity and public acclaim, Jackie appeared to enjoy herself immensely, perhaps because, as First Ladies historian Kati Marton has suggested, "India's flamboyance, the colors and the pomp, suited her." Besides, it must have been flattering, even for the famous and glamorous wife of the President of the United States, to hear adoring crowds welcome her as *Ameriki Rani,* "Queen of America." ❧

Jacqueline Kennedy makes a stop at the Taj Mahal on March 15, 1962, during a trip to India and Pakistan.

July 17, 1962

Send to Arthur
then have him return it to you
to file

Dear Jackie:

I am glad that you are so <u>delighted</u> with the Bryan-Salinger
tale. I hadn't realized that the author was Joe Bryan's son.
As for me, I have been swimming more lately, but enjoying it less.

Jim Babb has returned from Europe and we talked this
morning about the White House Library. We are arranging
to meet in New York early in August. I will try to get
Lyman Butterfield and Julian Boyd along at the same time.

I enclose a letter from Breeden of the <u>National Geographic</u>
raising a question about the Presidents' Book. My own view
is that we should stick to the idea of two pages to each
President and sell the book for seventy-five cents. I cannot
believe that the problem of making change presents such an
insuperable difficulty. To allot four pages to each President
would make the book much more of a production than you
originally envisaged. I would be grateful if you could let me
know your own thoughts on this question.

I hope you are enjoying the sun and breeze from which I have
with such difficulty torn myself away.

Wasn't it terrible about Peggy Talbott?

Much love,

Arthur Schlesinger, Jr.

Mrs. Kennedy
Hyannis Port, Massachusetts

I told Janet Felton
to send Babb
+ Boyd + Butterfield
copies of Library
Press Release which
wasn't printed
— so they will all
know — especially
Bibb — where I
stand on library +
I don't want a lot
of priceless books
we have to lock up
Its the content + a decent — preferably old
binding I care about — not the rarity of
the edition — though a carpet + those would be OK

We'll do it your way + sell it for $1.00
We will have 2 pages for each Pres. +
sell it for $1.00 as making change is
too difficult — The guidebook is a steal for $1.00 which everyone admits
This should make up a bit — + if people will pay 75¢ they will pay $1.00 — also
written by you gives it value — they are

OVER//

Arthur Schlesinger Jr. *to* Jacqueline Kennedy

Washington, D.C. · *July 17, 1962*

JACQUELINE KENNEDY'S LOVE FOR THE ARTS IS WELL KNOWN. Less often acknowledged is the fact that she loved books, too—not just reading them but making them. ❧ As a child, she wrote stories and essays, a few of which were published. In high school, she drew cartoons for the school newspaper. Later, she entered a *Vogue* magazine contest that required her to create a theme and prepare the layout—including a full slate of articles and illustrations—for an entire issue, then put together an advertising campaign to promote it. She won the contest, but her

mother refused to allow her to accept the prize, a stint in *Vogue's* editorial offices in New York and Paris.

She finally made it to Paris in 1951, when she and her sister traveled across Europe. After the trip, they produced a charming words-and-pictures journal of their experiences (Jackie made the drawings, both sisters wrote the text) that was later published under the title *One Special Summer*. Still drawn to journalism, Jackie took a job as a writer and photographer for a Washington newspaper, a job that resulted in a life-changing interview with a young senator from Massachusetts named John Kennedy. As Senator Kennedy's wife, she helped draft his speeches and performed editing chores for his Pulitzer Prize-winning book *Profiles in Courage,* and during the 1960 presidential campaign, she wrote a column called "Campaign Wife" that was distributed by the Democratic Party.

As part of the First Lady's headline-making renovation of the Executive Mansion in the 1960s, she conceived and oversaw the production of *The White House: An Historic Guide.* In her foreword she revealed that the guidebook had originally been planned

for children but was later targeted to a wider audience in the belief "that it never hurts a child to read something that may be above his head, and that books written down for children often do not awaken a dormant curiosity. . . ." The book became a best-seller.

When historian Arthur Schlesinger, Jr., wrote this letter to the First Lady, he had been involved with the Kennedy Administration for about a year, working as a special assistant in the White House. In the summer of 1962, he and Mrs. Kennedy were involved in a couple of book-related projects. One had to do with the expansion of the White House library, and the First Lady's handwritten note indicates that she has firm ideas about what kinds of books should be acquired: "I don't want a lot of priceless books we have to lock up," she writes. "It's the content & a decent—preferably old—binding I care about—not the rarity of the edition. . . ."

The second project involves a so-called Presidents' Book they want to produce with the National Geographic Society, which had published the White House guidebook. Because of her family's desire to respect her well-known passion for privacy, examples of Mrs. Kennedy's handwriting are rarely displayed, a fact that makes these pages particularly interesting. With the firmness and attention to detail that must have served her well as an editor, she deals with everything from how much the book should cost ("We will . . . sell it for $1.00 as making change is too difficult") to how its pages should be laid out. "For aesthetic reasons I want Pres picture to take up whole left page," she says. She generously leaves it to Schlesinger to decide how many words of text will be allotted to each President, but she has an opinion about that, too: "I think just 2 pages is so much easier. . . ."

The Presidents' Book never made it into print. Arthur Schlesinger went on to win the Pulitzer Prize and a National Book Award in 1966 for *A Thousand Days: John F. Kennedy in the White House,* which is still considered the definitive history of the Kennedy Administration. He maintained a close friendship with the former First Lady, often escorting her to movies and restaurants in New York.

As for Jacqueline Kennedy herself, after her marriage to Greek shipping tycoon Aristotle Onassis ended with his death in 1975, she worked as an editor for two major publishing houses, often writing forewords for the volumes she helped produce. Despite—or perhaps because of—her lifelong involvement in designing and editing books, she never got around to something she once said she really wanted to do: She never wrote a novel. ❦

Presidential historian Arthur Schlesinger, Jr., escorts Jacqueline Kennedy to the preview of a film on January 27, 1967.

Want object to price — you tell Mr

Breeden all this

II — Now I have a second thought — For aesthetic reasons
I want Pres picture to take up whole left page

So that will give you only one page of text —
the same size as W.H. guidebook — which
isn't much — & rather reduces you to firing
out facts like a biographical dictionary —

If we have 2 extra pages on each Pres — you would
only have 3/4 a page to write as we could toss in enormous
illustrations of their birthplaces etc. That is about 625
words — in the Nat Geog 2 column way —

If that is enough — go ahead with my plan — If you want
more words — we can have 4 pages & mostly fill it up
with pictures — I think just 2 pages is so much
easier — You can learn so much more at a glance
+ it just gets confusing + people not really interested want bother
to absorb all — So YOU make final decision

April 9, 1963

My dear Mrs. Kennedy:

Thank you very much for your note of the 7th. I completely agree with you that the window treatment is poor in both the new Executive Office Building and in the Courts Building planned for Lafayette Square. At the time John Warnecke made the presentation to us last fall, I told him that I did not like the window design and asked him to change it. The sketches shown in the AIA Journal for January are taken from the original plan and, therefore, they do not reflect any changes that have been worked on since that time. I have called John and he will be glad to fly to Washington on any one of the following days: April 29 and 30 and May 1, 2, and 3. If you will have your secretary call me, giving me the date that you prefer, I will be very happy to set up the meeting. For your convenience, I would suggest that we come to the White House if this is agreeable to you.

I also fully agree with you that the gardens and trees originally planned for this Square must be retained in the final plan and I will be talking with John about this prior to our meeting.

John assures me that he can have the plans complete for the new Executive Office Building and the Courts Building by early fall of this year. We are, therefore, planning to call for bids for these two buildings in October or November, with the construction period estimated to be between 24 and 30 months.

I have before the Bureau of the Budget a prospectus, which will require Congressional approval, for the restoration of the facades including the construction of replacement buildings fronting on Jackson Place and restoration of the Court of Claims Building. As soon as we receive a firm estimate of cost from John for the Executive Office Building and the Courts Building, we will be able to determine how much additional money will be required to do the balance of the work and this will be supplied to the Bureau of the Budget, enabling us to then transmit the prospectus to the Congress.

BERNARD BOUTIN *to* JACQUELINE KENNEDY

Washington, D.C. • April 9, 1963

LAFAYETTE SQUARE, ORIGINALLY KNOWN AS THE PRESIDENT'S PARK and located across Pennsylvania Avenue from the White House, was for many years the leafy centerpiece of Washington's most prestigious neighborhood. The square's north side was anchored by Benjamin Latrobe's elegant little St. John's Church, while its east and west flanks were lined with the handsome homes of Cabinet members, ambassadors, and leaders of society. ❧ The historic character of the square remained largely intact until the late 1950s, when it became a target. The federal government needed office space, and Lafayette Square seemed the perfect site. Almost all of the historic structures were slated for demolition, with modern office buildings to rise in their place.

Instead of being lost, however, Lafayette Square became the site of a major preservation triumph. The guiding force behind this dramatic turnaround was the square's best known resident, Jacqueline Kennedy. The First Lady's well-informed interest in American history and culture, which had already spurred a sweeping restoration of the interiors at the White House, convinced her that the square should not be sacrificed in the name of "progress."

With the advice of highly placed friends and contacts in the architectural and cultural communities, including David Finley, director of the National Gallery of Art, she enlisted architect John Carl Warnecke to find a way to provide the needed office space without destroying the character of the square. It was a challenging assignment, but Warnecke eventually produced an imaginative plan that preserved the 19th-century facades of the low-rise buildings facing the square and placed a matching pair of multistory red-brick office buildings behind them.

Among those most heavily involved in the Lafayette Square project was Bernard Boutin, head of the General Services Administration, the "landlord" agency that manages government buildings. This letter from Boutin reveals the extent of the First Lady's involvement in every detail of the project, from the restoration of the historic facades to the landscaping of the square itself, the construction of an underground parking garage and the design of the windows in the new office buildings. She played an active role in reviewing and fine-tuning every aspect of the design, and her attendance at meetings of the Commission of Fine Arts doubtless smoothed the way for the commission's final approval of the plans.

Warnecke later said that Mrs. Kennedy hoped to "change not only the minds of the world's leading architects but the actual direction of architecture in the United States"—and, to a great extent, she did. ❧

Sunday Noon
December 1, 1963

Dear Jackie:

How could you possibly find that extra moment — that extra ounce of strength to call me Thanksgiving evening.

You have been magnificent and have won a warm place in the heart of history.

I only wish things could be different — that I didn't have to be here.

But the Almighty has willed differently, and now Lady Bird and I need your help.

You have for now and for always our warm, warm love,

Affectionately,

Lyndon

Lyndon B. Johnson *to* Jacqueline Kennedy

Washington, D.C. • December 1, 1963

THEY COULD HARDLY HAVE BEEN MORE UNLIKE. Jacqueline Kennedy was raised in privilege, went to the best schools, and moved easily with the horsey set. Lyndon Johnson grew up in the hardscrabble farmland of Texas, where you rode a horse because you couldn't afford a car. She spoke in a breathy near-whisper; he often seemed to be bellowing even when he wasn't. She liked art and music and French cuisine; he liked politics. She charmed; he bullied. Little wonder that she found him crude and intimidating at first, and wasn't

particularly pleased when he became her husband's Vice President. But gradually she grew to appreciate his style, respect him, even like him.

In the terrible days after her husband's assassination in 1963, days when her stoic composure made her an icon of grace and grief, the new President reached out to the former First Lady. They spoke on the telephone several times in the first few days after Johnson took office. In one conversation he joshed her a bit: ". . . you females got a lot of courage that we men don't have. And so we have to rely on you and depend on you. . . . You've got the President relying on you! And this is not the first one you've had!"

In this note, however, there is no joshing. The pain is still too deep. We don't know what prompted Johnson to write it. He refers to having received a Thanksgiving telephone call from Jackie, but we don't know the details. Maybe it was sheer political pragmatism that prompted this note, or maybe it was merely an off-the-cuff gesture with little thought behind it, who knows? The latter seems unlikely: The tone is so gentle, the emotions so

heartfelt, that it can only be—must be—the simple, sincere expression of one human being reaching out to another.

There's not much to it, really. He tells her she has been "magnificent" and has "won a warm place in the heart of history." There's a rueful note near the end—"I only wish things could be different and I didn't have to be here"—before his closing assurance of love and affection.

In addition to being a compelling link with a traumatic historical event, the letter is an instructive reminder of the challenge of preserving fragile historical documents. The letter shown here, from the archives of the Lyndon B. Johnson Library in Austin, Texas, is a Thermofax copy of the original handwritten note. Thermofax, a predecessor of our current photocopy process, has proved to be very unstable, as indicated by the fading that has made portions of this letter almost illegible. According to the LBJ Library archivist, the print on this and other Thermofax copies will eventually disappear completely.

The feeling behind the words, however, will resonate forever. ✸

Beloved —

You are as
brave a man as
Harry Truman — or FDR
— or Lincoln. You
can go on to find
some peace, some
achievement amidst
all the pain. You
have been strong,
patient, determined
beyond any words
of mine to express.

Bird

Lady Bird Johnson *to* Lyndon B. Johnson

Washington, D.C. • August 1964

T HIS INTENSELY PERSONAL NOTE reminds us that the role of wife and supporter of her husband is one of the most important—and most demanding—of the many roles a First Lady is expected to play. ❧ Lyndon Johnson had a well-earned reputation as a man who thrived on the rough-and-tumble atmosphere of politics. But those close to him knew that he also had, as one historian wrote, "a huge, unappeasable hunger to be loved" and a deep-seated need for reassurance and encouragement. With the approach of the 1964 election, that need grew stronger. ❧ He had been in

office for only nine months—a period of whirlwind activity that largely reshaped the nation's political and social landscape. He helped Americans begin to heal from the trauma of President Kennedy's assassination, set in motion the array of programs that would create what he called The Great Society, declared "unconditional war on poverty," and persuaded Congress to pass the most sweeping civil rights legislation in the nation's history.

Each day's news brought fresh thunderbolts: On the morning of August 4, Johnson was told that for the second time in two days, North Vietnamese torpedo boats had attacked American ships in the Gulf of Tonkin, and on that same day, in a heart-stopping convergence of momentous events on opposite sides of the globe, he received word that the bodies of three civil rights workers missing since June had been found in Mississippi.

Confronting this assault of threats and uncertainties, Johnson wondered whether he was up to the challenge of being President for four more years. Lady Bird Johnson, who was not only his wife

but also his closest adviser, sought to calm his doubts with this letter. She sows the letter with adulatory adjectives: "brave," "strong," "patient," "determined." Knowing that her husband idolizes Abraham Lincoln, Franklin D. Roosevelt, and Harry Truman, she tells him that he is a worthy successor to them. To quit now would be "wrong for your country," but the final decision is his to make, and she will support him, no matter what: "I am not afraid of Time or lies or losing money or defeat."

Apparently, the First Lady's words had precisely the effect she intended. His misgivings laid to rest, Johnson made a triumphant appearance at the Democratic Convention in Atlantic City, accepting his party's nomination with a rousing speech that sketched the principal elements of the ambitious social and educational programs he intended to enact. Then, buoyed by the cheers of his supporters as well as the reassurances of his wife, he waged a vigorous campaign against the Republican candidate, Senator Barry Goldwater, and won the election by the second largest margin in history. ❧

NAME Jacque McKone
SUBJECT 4th Grade
DATE Oct. 4, 1964

Dear Mrs. Johnson,
My name is Jacque, I'm 9, and I
live in Lawler, Iowa. The reason
I called on you is becauses my
birthday was October 2, 64.
Saturday I got a bird from
my Mom + Dad. Today I
named it Lady Bird.
in memory of you and your
family. Right now I am
siting writing to you. and
at the same time wathing
Lady Bird. I put a
miorr in front of her
and she's going wild. Someday
we will come to see you.
Well by now.

Love in
Christ
Jacque

Jacque McKone *to* Lady Bird Johnson

Lawler, Iowa · October 4, 1964

CHILDREN ARE ALMOST ALWAYS FUN TO HAVE AROUND. For a busy First Lady in challenging and often stressful times, a letter from a child can provide welcome contact with the "real" world, and maybe provoke a smile. ❧ Lady Bird Johnson had a lot on her plate in the fall of 1964. While racial turmoil flared across the South and increased tensions in Vietnam led to a big increase in the number of American ground troops, a bitterly fought presidential campaign entered its final weeks. Determined to play an active role in her husband's reelection, Lady Bird launched an unprecedented

whistle-stop tour that took her through eight states in four days, exposing her to considerable heckling and firmly establishing her credentials as an articulate speaker and effective campaigner.

Through it all, the First Lady had to keep doing what she had done for 30 years:

humoring, soothing, and encouraging the rough, demanding, egocentric, larger-than-life man who was her husband. One of Johnson's law school classmates once told him, "The best day's work you ever did was the day you persuaded her to marry you." He knew it, of course, knew very well how much he needed her, but if anything, that only made her job harder.

This letter has nothing to do with any of that. In it, Jacque McKone reports that she got a bird for her birthday and has named it Lady Bird. Apparently the bird, like the President's wife, has a lot of energy: "I put a miorr in front of her," Jacque writes, "and she's going wild." We can only hope the First Lady didn't notice—or didn't mind—that the drawing makes her namesake look like roadkill.

One last thing about the nine-year-old author of this letter: She had been experimenting with cool ways to spell her name, but after Mrs. Johnson addressed her as "Master Jacque," she went back to the spelling she started with: Jackie. ❧

Jacque McKone, pictured on her grandfather's farm, wanted the First Lady "to know she had a friend out in the world."

March 10, 1965

Dear Mrs. Johnson,

Our group became very concerned last fall with the slow deterioration of property in our neighborhood.

We decided to begin with our school and try to beautify the grounds in the hopes that this would radiate out into the entire elementary school district.

Dutch Elm disease had claimed many of our trees, so with the help of our parks department we had locust and maple trees planted. This spring lilac bushes and barberry shrubs will be added.

The Men's Garden Club is going to replant the lawn; and work with the children in planting flowers.

This used to be a middle income area, now because of urban renewal there are many families in the area receiving welfare assistance. The adults are apathetic about their surroundings and their children show this through a lack of respect or responsibility for property.

We are planning assemblies with the children and a school picnic at the end of the term, but feel our children need even more of an incentive.

We felt a letter from our First Lady to the boys and girls about keeping their little corner of America beautiful would be of great help in instilling that special spark of civic pride that's needed here.

Mrs. Johnson, we will greatly appreciate any assistance you can give us.

Sincerely,

Lila Wright

(Mrs. Charles) Lila Wright
President
Merrick School Mother's Club

MERRICK SCHOOL MOTHERS CLUB
to LADY BIRD JOHNSON

Syracuse, New York • March 10, 1965

AUTO DISMANTLERS ASSOCIATION
to LADY BIRD JOHNSON

Los Angeles, California • April 5, 1965

CHRONICLERS OF LADY BIRD JOHNSON'S YEARS in the White House usually assert that her husband was her career. It's undeniably true that handling the rough-hewn Chief Executive—calming him down, bucking him up, reining him in—was a challenging task that could have occupied his wife's every waking moment. She needed a bigger outlet for her energy and interests, however, and she recognized that the visibility and prestige of her position gave her an opportunity to do something meaningful in an area that meant a great deal to her. ❦

Mrs. Johnson once acknowledged that for better or worse, a First Lady does not have a clearly written job description. Nonetheless, she added, "when she gets the job, a podium is there if she cares to use it. I did." She used her brightly lit podium to promote what became her "signature" cause: a widely publicized and highly popular campaign to make America beautiful. She always disliked the "beautification" label, feeling that it trivialized her motivation as well as the positive results it sparked. She was right: The beautification campaign was far more than a simplistic appeal to make things pretty for pretty's sake.

As America's inner cities became enclaves of disinvestment and deterioration in the 1960s, crime rates soared and the mean

Bill Crawford's 1965 cartoon satirized Lady Bird Johnson's effort to rid the country of highway billboards.

streets often exploded in violence. The now-discredited program known as Urban Renewal sought to remedy the situation by razing the so-called blighted areas to make way for shiny new office towers and housing complexes, but Mrs. Johnson suggested there were things "ordinary" people could do to bring a new, more positive spirit to struggling communities. "Where flowers bloom, so does hope," she proclaimed, and people took the message to heart. Flowers bloomed, sometimes in the unlikeliest places, and they're still blooming.

Lady Bird's legacy is particularly vivid in Washington, D.C., where springtime brings an annual explosion of color to the Potomac riverfront and parks throughout the nation's capital. But she was determined that the benefits of her beautification crusade not be confined to big cities that draw crowds of tourists, so she urged citizens in every community, big or small, to do what they could to make their streets and neighborhoods more attractive.

This letter from the Merrick School Mothers Club indicates that her suggestion took root—quite literally—in at least one community. Lila Wright tells the First Lady that the club's concern over the deterioration of their neighborhood led them to beautify the school grounds "in the hopes that this would radiate out into the entire elementary school district." She reports that they've planted locust and maple trees, lilac and barberry bushes will soon go into the ground, and they're planning assemblies and a picnic to teach children how to take responsibility for their community. It's exactly the kind of grassroots action that the beautification campaign was all about, and Mrs. Johnson's response

heaped praise all around: "I hope you will remember that your achievements in Syracuse are enhancing the entire Nation, and contributing to a better life for your fellow men."

As she traveled to almost every state to promote her campaign, the First Lady couldn't help noticing that many of the nation's highways needed attention, too. She persuaded the President to push for passage of the Highway Beautification Act of 1965, which called for tighter control of outdoor advertising along federal roadways and required that junkyards and other examples of visual blight be screened or removed. Not everyone was pleased.

In his letter to the First Lady, the president of the Auto Dismantlers Association of Southern California points out that his colleagues are pillars of the community: They are active in civic affairs, they pump money into the local economy, and they provide an essential service. He admits, however, that their work sites "do offend the public taste," and here's the good news: The auto dismantlers want to clean up their act (along with their junkyards), and they hope Lady Bird will invite them to participate in an upcoming White House conference on natural beauty.

In California, a grove of majestic redwoods now bears Lady Bird's name, as do a riverside park in Washington, D.C., and the acclaimed Wildflower Center in Austin, Texas. The most fitting tribute of all, however, may be this one: When Mrs. Johnson received an award from the National Building Museum, each guest at the presentation ceremony was given some wildflower seeds and tulip bulbs to take home and plant. *

Auto Dismantlers Association

OF SOUTHERN CALIFORNIA

April 5, 1965

PRESIDENT
TERRY FISKIN
Terry's Auto Parts
2211 E. Anaheim Blvd.
Wilmington, Calif.
775-3992

1ST VICE PRESIDENT
HERB LIEBERMAN
Lakenor Auto Salvage
10924 S. Norwalk Blvd.
Santa Fe Springs, Calif.
RAymond 3-4341

2ND VICE PRESIDENT
JERRY SPECTOR
S & S Auto Salvage
7833 E. Compton Blvd.
Paramount, Calif.
NEvada 6-2216

SECRETARY
ROBERT MAXFIELD
Maxfield's Auto Parts
2856 Cherry Blvd.
Long Beach, Calif.
GArfield 7-9949

TREASURER
ED BEARD
Hiway 39 Auto Wrecking
10181 Stanton Ave.
Stanton, Calif.
TAylor 8-3340

PAST PRESIDENTS
Irv Greenwald
Larry Schwartz
William Byrtus
Harvey Schulberg
Stanley Hepner
Abe Cohen
Morris Levy
Sam Cohen
Alvin Levine
George Ratcliffe
Norman Port
George Friedland
Louis Friedland
Sol Gurian
Harry Pava
Larry Simon
Sol Levine
R. E. Franklin
J. Clayman°
J. Pearlman°
Morris Scher°

LIFE MEMBERS
Joe Werzel
Wm. L. Sweet

BOARD OF DIRECTORS
Sam Adlen
Don Byrtus
Ken Clark
Mike Huniu
Dennis Irving
Gilbert Jacobs
Al Lieberman
Paul Okyle
Lou Periof
Robert Platt
John Rose
Harvey Sklar
Leo Spiwak
Joe Solomon
Linc Urdangen
Irv Weiss

Mrs. Lyndon B. Johnson
THE WHITE HOUSE
Washington D.C.

Dear Mrs. Johnson:

We are deeply concerned over your sincere criticism of the appearance of many of the nation's auto dismantling yards. For this reason we of the Auto Dismantlers Association of Southern California have launched a major industry "face lift".

This industry is well aware of the problems it faces and the problems it poses for civic authorities. The business of operating a dismantling yard is a legitimate enterprise which does not constitute a dangerous business or one which is known to be inherently injurious or harmful to the public.

We admit, however, that many do offend the aesthetic taste and the Auto Dismantlers Association of Southern California is proud to offer its cooperation in a wholehearted effort to rectify this situation.

Our entire membership is pledged to assist in implementing the President's "Let's Beautify America" program. We should like to participate in the White House Conference on Natural Beauty scheduled to take place in May, and humbly request an invitation to attend.

I would like to point out that local auto dismantlers are men who have been in business for many years and operate businesses of some substance. They are active in community affairs. Their expenditures for inventory, labor and services are almost all made in their hometowns. And most important, without the auto dismantlers, the community would be faced with a virtually insoluable hard goods disposal problem.

I think all of us now realize that what we need is better understanding of the functions of the average auto dismantler and closer cooperation among the dismantlers, community officials and the planners designing future civic developments.

Respectfully yours,

Terry Fiskin
PRESIDENT

TF:ha

EXECUTIVE DIRECTOR   **ED LEVEN,** 160 South Robertson Boulevard, Beverly Hills, California, OL 5-5536

LEGAL COUNSELOUR   **JOSEPH L. ALTAGEN,** Altagen & Rubin, 1813 Wilshire Boulevard, Los Angeles, California, HU 3-6262

August 11, 1967.
67 North St
Hingham, Mass.

Dear Mrs Johnson,

I would just like to
Briefly tell you what
the effect of the Headstart
Program has had on my
Son Ronald 5½ years.
He Has one week left
to finish the program in
our town. And the past
Seven weeks he has become
a different child. he has
always been difficult to Handle

GENA GEEDY *to* LADY BIRD JOHNSON

Hingham, Massachusetts • August 11, 1967

O F THE MANY INITIATIVES LAUNCHED to support the Johnson Administration's War on Poverty, few have provided greater or more lasting benefit than Project Head Start, established in 1965 to improve educational opportunities for preschool children in underprivileged families. From the start, Lady Bird Johnson was the ambitious program's most passionate and highly visible champion. ✻ In this letter, a Massachusetts mother named Gena Geedy tells the First Lady what Head Start has done for her five-year-old son, Ronald. He's always been

a handful, but Head Start has taught him that school can be a fun place, learning is essential, and a little discipline is good for you, too. He's "become a different child," his mother says, and then, to underscore the point, she says it a second time: "Ronnie is a new child."

All three of Geedy's children and one of her grandchildren participated in Head Start. Ronald, the kid who was "difficult to handle," is all grown up now, a businessman with two children of his own. Reaching more than 900,000 children in 2007, Head Start is still going strong. ✻

Lady Bird Johnson visits a Head Start classroom at the Kemper School in Washington, D.C., on March 19, 1968.

1192 Ridge Dr.
Austin, Texas 78721
March 13, 1968

Dear Mrs. Johnson,
    Thank you for signing,
my certificate in the head
start. Now, I am going
to Pease School and in the
3rd grade. I'm nine years
old. And didn't think
that was nice of Miss
Eartha Kitt to say all
those

Bessie Mae Hicks *to* Lady Bird Johnson

Austin, Texas · March 13, 1968

BY 1968, THE WAR IN VIETNAM HAD BECOME A DIVISIVE, pervasive presence in almost every aspect of American life, dominating political debate on Capitol Hill as well as cocktail-party chatter in homes from coast to coast. ❧ On January 18, Lady Bird Johnson invited 50 prominent women to the White House for a discussion of juvenile delinquency and other issues affecting urban youth. The conversation proceeded smoothly at first, but then singer/actress Eartha Kitt rose to her feet and gave the First Lady a piece of her

mind. "Boys I know across the nation feel it doesn't pay to be a good guy," she said. "They don't want to go to school because they are going to be snatched from their mothers to be shot in Vietnam. . . . I am a mother and I know the feeling of having a baby come out of my guts. I have a baby and then you send him off to war. No wonder the kids rebel and take pot. And, Mrs. Johnson, in case you don't understand the lingo, that's marijuana!"

The shaken Lady Bird later wrote that she felt "a wave of mounting disbelief. Can this be true? Is this a nightmare?" Recovering her composure, she replied, "Because there is a war on, that doesn't give us a free ticket not to try to work for better things. . . . I have not lived the background that you have, nor can I speak as passionately or as well, but we must keep our eyes and our hearts and our energies fixed on constructive areas and try to do something that will make this a happier, better educated land." Though there were rumors that Mrs. Johnson had been reduced to tears, most people present felt that she had

handled a difficult situation with admirable aplomb.

Kitt's outburst made headlines all over the country and prompted a rush of messages to the White House. One of them was this letter from a nine-year-old girl in the First Lady's own home state of Texas. Bessie Mae Hicks mostly wants to thank Mrs. Johnson for signing her Head Start certificate, but she can't help adding that she "didn't think it was nice of Miss Eartha Kitt to say all those things about you in public." The First Lady doesn't deserve this kind of abuse, Bessie Mae insists: "I think you are a nice person. You're a kind person too."

Eartha Kitt paid a high price for her outspokenness: She was blacklisted by venues in which she had previously headlined, and she later learned that she was the subject of covert investigations by the FBI and the CIA. Unable to find work in this country, she spent a decade performing in Europe. In 1978, she finally returned to the Broadway stage and was welcomed back to the White House by President Jimmy Carter, who said simply, "Welcome home, Eartha." ❧

August 3, 1974

Dear Mrs. Marrero,

It is a pleasure to send a warm welcome and congratulations to a new American citizen! Your beautiful letter was inspiring to all our family.

We were particularly happy to learn of your loyalty and your affiliation with the Republican Party. Your selection of it at this time is an expression of faith and confidence and is a reflection of the positive spirit which made our country great. The high regard which you express for the President and with which you generously credit your decision means very much to all of us. We especially value your appreciation for the Viet Nam resolution and your dedication in writing to your Congressman. Your friendship is a special quantity which we will treasure always.

With gratitude for your thoughts and prayers and with our very best wishes,

Sincerely,

Mrs. Alicia Marrero
530 South West Eighth Court
Miami, Florida 33130

AH/mlb

Pat Nixon *to* Mrs. Alicia Marrero

Washington, D.C. • August 3, 1974

WHEN YOU STUDY PHOTOGRAPHS OF HER FACE in the final years of her term as First Lady, it's hard to remember that Pat Nixon was once a lively redhead who worked as a movie extra. Then she met Richard Nixon and embarked on a 30-year career as the wife of a politician who was a lightning rod for controversy. ❧ By the summer of 1974, it was all falling apart. People who opposed the war in Vietnam, people who were furious over the Watergate political espionage scandal, people who simply hated her husband—all of them turned their anger on her, calling her "Plastic Pat" and often shouting horrible things at her. Even more damaging, her husband sometimes seemed to have relegated her to a marginal role in his life as he engaged in a single-minded pursuit of political power and the respect of his peers.

Television reporter Diane Sawyer, who worked in the White House during this period, has said that the Nixons "were locked in this dance of unhappiness. He felt indebted to her, and felt that he had won her and then imprisoned her."

The First Lady was trapped in a world she had never wanted and didn't like, and her feelings of betrayal and disappointment showed in her face. Her eyes took on a haunted (or was it *hunted*?) look. She smiled when she had to—she had a warm personality, genuinely liked people, and did well in public appearances—but the smiles grew so transparent that you could almost see the darker emotions that quivered behind them. Looking at photographs of her from this time, you can't avoid using tragic adjectives to describe her: sad, hurt, wounded, broken.

Even as the Nixon Administration crumbled in deception and disgrace all around her, she never neglected her duties as First Lady. She was especially conscientious about her correspondence, sometimes spending four or five hours a day in an effort to ensure that every person who wrote to her received a prompt response.

One of those to whom she wrote was a new American citizen named Alicia Marrero. After conveying "a warm welcome and congratulations," Mrs. Nixon expresses special gratitude for Marrero's decision to join the Republican Party, describing it as "an expression of faith and confidence . . . and a reflection of the positive spirit which made our country great."

What makes the letter remarkable is its date: August 3, 1974. It was Pat Nixon's final week as First Lady. Just six days after she encouraged Alicia Marrero to keep believing in the promise of America, she boarded a helicopter with her husband and left the White House. As they lifted into the air, the ex-President heard her murmur, to no one in particular, "It's so sad. It's so sad." ❧

Dear Mrs. Ford:

Number one, we both have the same name, we have similar looks and are approximately the same age.

My problem is that I am also a relatively known celebrity "wife" "Tennessee Ernie", being my husband.

I have never had a problem with my credit cards or cashing a check, now all this has changed!

I am now accused of being "You," !! or fraudulently using your "name". One minute I am fawned upon and the next time I am hauled to the managers' office to expose all my damned credit cards, plus drivers permit (with picture). I will admit my picture on the drivers' permit looks like a picture of some pathetic creature from a beleagured nation.

Thank you for all the fun & hate you for being a size 8.

Sincerely,
Betty Ford

BETTY FORD *to* BETTY FORD

Address Unknown · September 1974

ALARMING NEWS STORIES HAVE MADE US INCREASINGLY AWARE that identity theft is a major scourge of 21st-century life, a cyber-plague that threatens our economic well-being and our peace of mind. Actually, identity theft is hardly new. As this letter indicates, it was a serious issue as far back as 1974. ❧ Betty Ford has a problem, and it's Betty Ford. The woman who wrote this letter, Betty Ford #1, lives in California and is married to a famous entertainer. Betty #2, to whom the letter is addressed, lives in Washington, D.C., and is married to the President

of the United States. Here's the problem: People can't accept the notion that there are *two* Betty Fords, so they keep accusing the first one of trying to pass herself off as the second one.

Life used to be good for Betty #1. As the wife of Tennessee Ernie Ford—an affable singer who cut several hit records, including the blockbuster "Sixteen Tons," played sold-out concert engagements, made guest appearances on *I Love Lucy,* and eventually had his own TV show—she was able to cut a pretty wide swath through the retail landscape of southern California. But now that Betty #2 has moved into the White House, Betty #1 finds that shopping has become an exercise in frustration and embarrassment: "I am accused of . . . fraudulently using your name," she writes. "One minute I am fawned upon and the next . . . I am hauled to the managers' office to expose all my damned credit cards. . . ." As if that weren't sufficiently humiliating, some shopkeepers have the effrontery to ask her to produce a photo ID—and the

picture on her driver's license makes her look like "some pathetic creature from a beleagured nation."

She has one more bone to pick with Betty #2, and she saves it for her final sentence: "[I] hate you for being a size 8." Oh, the horror. ❧

Betty Ford, the wife of Tennessee Ernie Ford, pictured here in the early 1970s, was often confused with the First Lady.

MARIA VON TRAPP
STOWE, VERMONT 05672

August 12, 1975.

Dear Mrs. Ford:

You may have noticed what an outrage was raised all over the country by your flippant remark on television.

By way of introduction I want you to know that I am "the real Maria from 'The Sound of Music.'" As such, I am very much in the limelight. All during the summer people come in busloads from around the country to meet me, take my picture and to get my autograph. I only say this that you may understand that I really meet hundreds of people every day, and I can assure you you have done great damage to your husband's political aspirations.

Both of you have lost a great deal of respect and good will among the people of the United States.

But aside from all this, do you realize how much harm you have done to the American family and to the American youth?

I pray that God will give you the necessary insight. Then please, Mrs. Ford, have the courage to step before the camera again and try to undo some of the damage. If it comes from your heart, people will believe you.

Sincerely yours,

Maria von Trapp

MARIA VON TRAPP *to* BETTY FORD

Stowe, Vermont • August 12, 1975

BETTY FORD ENJOYED BEING FIRST LADY, describing it as "like going to a party you're terrified of, and finding out to your amazement that you're having a good time." She especially relished the opportunity to express her views on important issues. As a proud feminist, she worked for passage of the Equal Rights Amendment. When she learned she had breast cancer and underwent a mastectomy, her candor inspired thousands of women. Admitting to a dependence on alcohol and pain medications, she founded the Betty Ford Center to help others overcome their addictions. ❧

On August 10, 1975, Mrs. Ford was interviewed on the popular television show *60 Minutes*. As was to be expected from a woman who believed that "being ladylike does not require silence," she spoke her mind freely, applauding the Supreme Court's decision in *Roe* v. *Wade*, admitting that she might try marijuana if she were young, and saying she wouldn't be surprised to learn that her daughter was having premarital sex.

After the interview, thousands of people wrote to the White House. Many supported Betty, one praising her as "one of the most beautifully contemporary and totally balanced people in public life." Others, however, shared the viewpoint of this letter from Maria von Trapp, whose life story inspired Rodgers and Hammerstein's *The Sound of Music*. In tones appropriate for a woman who has been a nun, governess, choirmaster, and refugee, she gives the First Lady a dressing-down for "flippant" remarks that have "done great damage to your husband's political aspirations," robbed her of "respect and good will among the people of the United States," and caused great harm "to the American family and . . . American youth."

President Ford estimated that his wife's remarks cost him 20 million votes, but *Newsweek* named her Woman of the Year, noting that, after Betty, a more traditional First Lady would be "a bit of a bore." ❧

Maria von Trapp submitted this "declaration of intention" to become a U.S. citizen on January 21, 1944.

LA CASA PACIFICA
SAN CLEMENTE, CALIFORNIA

May 23, 1975

Dear Betty –
    Pat and I thought
these pictures of you which
appeared on front page of
the L.A. Times were great!
    My favorite is the one
when you are shaking hands
with Ky. As I told Jerry on
the phone you have
classic features which come
across beautifully in profile.
    Keep up the good work –
But be sure both Jerry and
you get the rest and recreation
you need.
    It's a long, hard road.
Don't get too tired and Rockwell.
The Country needs you both.
Pat joins me in sending our best. Dick Nix

RICHARD NIXON *to* BETTY FORD

San Clemente, California • May 23, 1975

I T'S A LONG, HARD ROAD," RICHARD NIXON WRITES TO BETTY FORD, and if anyone has earned the right to be considered an expert on difficult journeys, it's the
only President in American history who resigned from the highest office in the
land. ❦ When this letter was written, less than a year had passed since that unfor-
gettable moment when a helicopter lifted the disgraced Nixon out of the White House
and into early retirement. In self-imposed exile at his San Clemente, California, home,
he brooded and read the newspapers. The headlines were dire: Saigon had fallen a few

weeks earlier, and 38 Americans had
been killed in the rescue of the merchant
ship *Mayaguez,* but when he spotted photographs of the First Lady on the front page
of the *Los Angeles Times,* he dashed off a note
to her.

It's a strange letter, even a little bit
creepy in places. He showers Betty with
compliments, telling her the photos
were "great" and adding that her "classic features . . . come across beautifully
in profile." Then, in what may be a veiled
acknowledgment of her cancer surgery a
few months earlier, he solicitously urges
her to "be sure both Gerry and you get
the rest and recreation you need" because
"the country *needs* you both."

What does it mean? Or are we doing
the ex-President an injustice by asking the question? A cynic might say that
Nixon is trying to stay on the good side
of the wife of President Ford, the man
whose controversial pardon saved him—
and the nation—from the agony of a
protracted and divisive impeachment.
A more generous reader might say that
Nixon is merely being nice. Perhaps the
truth lies somewhere in between.

Throughout the long roller-coaster
ride that was his political career, opponents and critics looked for reasons to
hate Richard Nixon and often didn't have
to look very far. They said he was vicious
and crude and underhanded, a whiner
who never forgot a slight and never
missed a chance to get back at those who
had wronged him. They lambasted him
as a ruthless opportunist who told whop-
ping lies and displayed a blithe disregard
for the niceties of the Constitution. They
accused him of mistreating his long-suf-
fering wife and ignoring her needs. They
called him "Tricky Dick" and pointed
out that he even *looked* sneaky. When he
insisted, "I am not a crook," they shouted
at the television screen, "Yes, you are!"

But, once in a while, the extremely
guarded and intensely secretive Nixon
allowed a bit of human warmth to show
through the thick defensive shell he had
built. That's what's on display—in a limited dose, admittedly, and only for a few
short paragraphs—in this letter from a
man who has risen and fallen impossibly
far and is trying to figure out how to put
himself back together. ❦

Dear Miss Betty Ford
My name is Roxie
Lee McCarty. My handle
on the CB is Freckels.
What is your handle.
And an eight. I have wrote
to the Presednt befor. What
is your favorit riceepe.
My Moms handel is
luchy lady and My Dads
is Mr. Clean and My
brother's handle is
Possun Ears What is your
daughters name? Well you
send me a picture of all
your famley please and
a picture of your dog.
I am glad that ford is
our presednt. I hope that
you like my letter. I am
in the third Grade I
live at Marion Ill 62959
Well you send my a
picture of your house
please. Well you please
anser my ?'s I have
to go now by
    Love,
        Roxie

ROXIE LEE MCCARTY *to* BETTY FORD

Marion, Illinois · June 1976

IN AN AGE WHEN WE CAN ENJOY INSTANTANEOUS COMMUNICATION with anyone, anytime, anywhere, it's hard to remember the excitement with which Americans in the 1970s embraced the citizens band radio. ❧ CB, as everyone called it, originated in the 1940s as a means of short-distance radio communications among citizens. As technological advances, especially the replacement of tubes with transistors, made CB radios smaller and more affordable, their use became more widespread, particularly among truckers, who found them useful in warning one another of police speed traps after the nationwide speed limit was dropped to 55 miles an hour in 1974. After a spate of movies and TV shows—you remember *Smokey and the Bandit, The Dukes of Hazzard, Convoy,* and *B.J. and the Bear,* don't you?—splashed CBs across the big theater screen and its smaller living-room counterpart, a full-fledged, pedal-to-the-metal CB craze erupted.

Suddenly, not only truckers but also architects and store managers and hairdressers and electricians were heard to say improbable things like "That's a big 10-4, good buddy" and "I've got your backdoor, do you copy?" Even more remarkably, people whose parents had given them all-American names like Bill and Jeff and Marge now sprouted "handles."

In this letter from June 1976, eight-year-old Roxie Lee McCarty of Marion, Illinois, uses a sheet of mercilessly cheerful stationery to tell "Miss Betty Ford" that the McCarty family is deeply involved in the CB fad. Everybody in the household, it seems, has a handle: Mom's is Lucky Lady, Dad's is Mr. Clean, and Brother's—for reasons that are not made clear—is Possum Ears. (Actually, Roxie Lee writes "Possun Ears." The prospect of communicating with the President's wife has doubtless set her nerves aflutter, but we know what she means.) As for the writer herself, her handle is Freckles, and it's easy to imagine why.

As it happened, the First Lady was already a bona fide CBer, having received her license a few weeks earlier. Not long after Roxie Lee wrote to her, the Seneca Social CBers of Geneva, New York, made Mrs. Ford an honorary member of their club, and she responded by assuring them (somewhat long-windedly) that she had "very much enjoyed this special area of communication" and was "proud to be associated with the fine group of Americans banded together in a common network of mutual support and assistance."

Later that summer, radio station WSBT in South Bend, Indiana, invited its listeners to come up with a suitable handle for the First Lady, and among those suggested were Top Banana's Momma, Queen Bee, Twinkle Toes, Betty Boots, and Lib Lady. Any of them would have been appropriate, but Betty had already picked one that was just right: First Mama. ❧

CAMBRIDGE SURVEY RESEARCH INCORPORATED

12-14 Mifflin Place Cambridge Massachusetts 02138 617/66
1775 Pennsylvania Avenue, N. W., Suite 1250
Washington, D. C. 20006   202/223-6345

Rosalynn —
Don't run against
your husband!
J

MEMORANDUM

TO   ROSALYNN CARTER

FROM   PATRICK H. CADDELL

RE   RECENT SURVEY FINDINGS

DATE   JULY 30, 1977

We conducted a survey after your recent Latin America
trip. Beyond looking at general reactions to you, we also
sought to measure reactions specifically to the trip and
your role as a representative of the President and the United
States. On the whole, the reactions were very, very favorable.

We began our examination by looking at Mrs. Carter's
favorable/unfavorable rating. As the table shows, she is
rated overwhelmingly favorable by the American public.
Indeed, it is a higher rating than we have found for recent
First Ladys. Her favorable rating is a shade below that
of the President with a lower unfavorable rating.

	Rosalynn Carter		Jimmy Carter
	Today	January	Today
Favorable	76%	56%	78%
Unfavorable	12	10	15
Can't rate	11	32	6
Never heard of	1	2	–

As the table shows, Mrs. Carter's rating has increased
greatly since January. Her favorable rating is up 20 points
while her unfavorable rating is only up 2 points. It is
clear that the American people are impressed with her early
performance as First Lady.

Patrick H. Caddell *to* Rosalynn Carter

Address Unknown • *July 30, 1977*

BEFORE A LETTER TO THE WHITE HOUSE REACHES ITS INTENDED RECIPIENT, it is usually scrutinized by a diligent legion of what one writer described as "the buffer people." Often, these reviewers scribble their own opinions and suggestions on the incoming letter, and in many cases, their notations are at least as engaging and enlightening as the original document. This memo is a case in point. ❧ When Rosalynn Carter moved into the White House as First Lady, she had already established herself as an equal and valued partner in her husband's business and political

endeavors. As a peanut farmer in Georgia, Jimmy Carter relied on his wife's bookkeeping skills to keep the family business running smoothly. When he was elected to the state senate, she not only took on an expanded role in managing the business but also handled much of the correspondence between her husband and his constituents. When he ran for governor, she overcame her initial stage fright to become an effective campaigner, and as mistress of the Governor's Mansion, she showed great poise and savvy in playing the public role that her position conferred on her.

In the White House, President Carter continued to rely on his wife's advice and assistance, and she responded enthusiastically by involving herself in political affairs to a much greater extent than any of her predecessors. She held weekly business lunches with the President and frequently sat in on Cabinet meetings, and in June 1977 she embarked on an extensive trip to Latin America, not merely visiting orphanages and artisans' workshops as previous First Ladies had done but officially representing her husband in substantive talks with heads of state. Critics complained that the First Lady was stepping into a job for which she had not been elected, but when she was questioned about her credentials in international diplomacy, she responded, "I am closer to the President of the United States than any person in the world."

This memo from Patrick Caddell, a pollster who served as a consultant to the Carter White House, summarizes the findings of a public-opinion survey undertaken soon after the First Lady's return from Latin America. As Caddell points out, the "very, very favorable" reactions make it "clear that the American people are impressed with [Mrs. Carter's] early performance as First Lady." More than three-fourths of those polled give her a thumbs-up—20 points higher than her rating six months earlier—while only 12 percent express an unfavorable opinion of her.

It's good news for the Carter Administration, but the fact that his wife's "unfavorable" rating is three points lower than his own may be what prompted the President to add an alarmed note: "Rosalynn: Don't run against your husband!" ❧

July 30, 1981

Dear Mrs. Reagan,

I have never in my life written a letter to a celebrity, not even to a teenage singing idol, but I have felt compelled to communicate my admiration of your portrayal of our First Lady to you personally.

During the election campaign of your husband, through the Inauguration you have displayed an elegance and charm that is uplifting to this wife and mother. I was especially proud of your representation of our country at the Royal Wedding. You displayed such good taste in your wardrobe, you looked

VICTORIA SCHMITT *to* NANCY REAGAN

Woodson, Texas • July 30, 1981

NANCY REAGAN MAY WELL HAVE BEEN the most widely criticized First Lady since Eleanor Roosevelt. People called her "Queen Nancy" and worried that she exerted too much influence over the hiring and firing of her husband's staff. They ridiculed her for consulting an astrologer to help her arrange the President's schedule. They accused her of failing to disclose the borrowing of expensive designer clothes, and maybe even keeping some of them. They complained that she spent too much money on new dishes and furniture for the White House and

that she maintained a "bloated, expensive East Wing staff." When she learned she had breast cancer and decided to have a mastectomy, they criticized her for not choosing a less radical surgical procedure. Political columnist William Safire, voicing the suspicions of many, went so far as to insist that she was deliberately misleading the public about her husband's deteriorating mental condition so that she could exercise power in his name like an "incipient Edith Wilson."

But—and it's a very big "but"—Mrs. Reagan was also one of the most widely admired presidential wives ever. This 1981 letter comes from one of her most ardent fans. Like so many others who pour out their feelings to movie stars and rock-and-roll musicians, Victoria Schmitt begins with a disclaimer: "I have never in my life written a letter to a celebrity, not even to a teenage singing idol. . . ." She feels compelled to write this one because she can no longer refrain from letting the First Lady know that one young woman in Texas admires just about everything about her.

She begins by praising the innate "elegance and charm" and good taste in clothes

that made Mrs. Reagan "an excellent addition to the beauty" of the recent wedding of Prince Charles and Lady Diana. But even more than superficial things like poise and social graces and good grooming, Victoria admires the First Lady for her unapologetic embodiment of the "role of a woman, wife and mother in our society." Victoria has "a wonderful husband who works hard" and "a wonderful, beautiful 16 month old baby boy," she writes, and she knows "if I don't give my full support to my husband and son . . . everyone's life would be very unhappy, especially mine."

It comes down to this: Victoria Schmitt wants to be a good wife and mother, and she applauds Nancy Reagan for encouraging her to realize that it's all right—no, much *more* than all right—to feel that way.

Lots of people shared Victoria Schmitt's high opinion of the First Lady. Six months after this letter was written, a Gallup poll named Nancy Reagan the most admired woman in the world. She finished ahead of First Lady Jackie Kennedy, U.S. Supreme Court Justice Sandra Day O'Connor, British Prime Minister Margaret Thatcher, and Mother Teresa. ✻

THE WHITE HOUSE

WASHINGTON

Dear Mrs. R.   Dec. 25 1981

I still don't feel right about your opening
an envelope instead of a gift package.

There are several much beloved women in
my life and on Christmas I should be giving them
gold, precious stones, perfume, furs and lace. I know
that even the best of these would still fall far
short of expressing how much these several
women mean to me and how empty my life
would be without them.

There is of course my "First Lady." She brings
so much grace and charm to whatever she
does that even stuffy, formal functions sparkle
and turn into fun times. Everything is done
with class. All I have to do is wash up and
show up.

There is another woman in my life who does
things I don't always get to see but I hear about
them and sometimes see photos of her doing
them. She takes an abandoned child in her arms
on a hospital visit. The look on her face only
the Madonna could match. The look on the child's
face is one of adoration. I know because I adore
her too.

She bends over a wheelchair or bed to
touch an elderly invalid with tenderness and
compassion just as she fills my life with warmth
and love.

There is another gal I love who is a neat
builder. If she were stuck three days in a
hotel room she'd manage to make it home sweet
home. She moves things around — looks at it —
straightens this and that and you wonder why

RONALD REAGAN *to* NANCY REAGAN

Washington, D.C. · *December 25, 1981*

Aboard Air Force One · *March 4, 1983*

AS A HOLLYWOOD ACTOR, Ronald Reagan never had a reputation as a great onscreen lover. In real life, however, he and First Lady Nancy Reagan starred in a love story that could have won Oscars. Reagan himself described it this way: "From the start, our marriage was like an adolescent's dream of what a marriage should be." ❧ When her stepson Michael was about to get married, Nancy offered some wise words of advice: "You'll never get in trouble if you say I love you at least once a day." These two letters from 1981 and 1983 indicate that the President

heartily agreed with her suggestion and fully understood the importance of letting his wife know exactly how he felt about her.

The first letter, which was written on Christmas Day, echoes FDR's frustration over what gift is most appropriate for his wife. It's especially tough, Reagan writes, because the woman in question is many people: As "my 'First Lady,'" she makes "stuffy, formal functions sparkle and turn into fun times." As a caring public figure, she "takes an abandoned child in her arms" or "bends over a wheelchair or bed to touch an elderly invalid with tenderness and compassion." As a "nest builder," she "straightens this and that and you wonder why it wasn't that way in the first place." As his companion at Rancho del Cielo, the Reagans' vacation retreat in California, she is fun "to sit by the fire with, or to ride with or just to be with." "I love the whole gang of you," he concludes, "so please always be there."

In the second letter, written on Air Force One on the couple's 31st wedding anniversary, the President who was called "the

Great Communicator" shares his feelings after a solitary two-day stay at the ranch: "I only love it when you are there. Come to think of it that's true of every place & every time. . . . I more than love you, I'm not whole without you. You are life itself to me. When you are gone I'm waiting for you to return so I can start living again." No studio scriptwriter could have said it better.

In her 1989 memoir, *My Turn*, Nancy Reagan wrote, "It would be far better and more realistic if the president's men included the first lady as part of their team. After all, nobody knows the president better than his wife. The president has a host of advisers to give him counsel on foreign affairs, the economy, politics and everything else. But not one of these people is there to look after him as an individual with human needs, a man of flesh and blood who must deal with the pressures of holding the most powerful position on earth."

She always insisted that she had no policy agenda of her own, no interest in establishing herself as an independent player in the high-stakes game of politics. As one biographer noted, "Nancy . . . served her husband, not the country. He was her career." She said as much in a 1967 letter to Ronnie: "Everything began with you, my whole life—so you'd better be careful and take care of yourself because there'd be nothing and I'd be no one without you."

She confided that she was often exasperated by her husband's refusal to recognize "anything evil in another human being." She decided it was up to her to be his protector, and she took up the role with what some called an excess of zeal, shielding him from anyone who didn't share her own views on what was in the best interests of the President and his legacy. The role

took on a new and greater urgency after Reagan was diagnosed with Alzheimer's disease in the 1990s. He lingered until 2004, but all through the shadowy final years, years that his daughter called "the long goodbye," observers noted that even on the days when he was most confused and uncommunicative, his face lit up when his wife walked into the room.

Of the many love letters Ronnie sent to Nancy, one of the simplest and truest says just one thing, I love you, but it repeats the three words over and over, in a column that runs from top to bottom of a sheet of White House stationery. The First Lady had it framed and kept it on her desk. ❧

President and Mrs. Reagan overlook Lake Lucky at Rancho del Cielo, near Santa Barbara, California, March 4, 1982.

 March 4 1983

Dear First Lady

I know tradition has it that on this morning I place 'cards – Happy Anniversary cards on your breakfast tray. But things are somewhat mixed up. I substituted a gift & delivered it a few weeks ago.

Still this is the day, the day that marks 31 years of such happiness as comes to few men. I told you once it was like an adolescents dream of what marriage should be like. That hasn't changed.

You know I love the ranch – but these last two days made it plain I only love it when you are there. Come to think of it that's true of every place & every time. When you aren't there I'm no place, just lost in time & space.

I more than love you, I'm not whole without you. You are life itsself to me. When you are gone I'm waiting for you to return so I can start living again.

Happy Anniversary & thank you for 31 wonderful years. I love you.
                    Your grateful husband.

March 19, 1982

Mrs. Nancy Reagan
The White House
1600 Pennsylvania Ave
Washington DC 20064

Dear Mrs. Reagan:

Recently, I listened to an interview of yours on the radio concerning drug abuse. You had at the time, just begun your campaign to discuss drug abuse with teen-ager. I've written to express an objection to something you said.

You said probably every teenager has tried marijuana at one time or another. Adults should not make the generalization that all teenagers are strongly influenced by their peers. Although this is true to an extent, there are a good many who are strong enough to prevail against the whims of others.

MARGARET SHOZDA *to* NANCY REAGAN

Landenberg, Pennsylvania • March 19, 1982

I N THE EARLY 1980S NANCY REAGAN BECAME deeply concerned about increasing drug use among young people, an epidemic that reportedly affected one out of three American households. At an appearance at a school in California, when a student told the First Lady how hard it was to deal with peer pressure to use drugs, she replied, "Just say NO! That's all you have to do." The phrase quickly entered the public lexicon. Stand-up comedians and talk-show hosts turned it into fodder for their jokes, but on a more positive note, thousands of "Just Say No" clubs were founded in schools across the country. ❦

Margaret Shozda heard all of the rhetoric, all of the alarming statistics, all of the

gloom-and-doom pronouncements that an entire generation was consigning itself to the hell of drug addiction, and in this letter from 1982 she issues an indignant two-word response: *Not me.* "I for one and all my closest friends have never tried marijuana," she tells Mrs. Reagan. "I am sure there are many others who also have no intention of doing so. I feel we deserve more credit than we are given."

The First Lady responded promptly, promising not to make easy generalizations about adolescent drug use. "Your letter made my day!" she wrote. "Thank you, and I will be more careful in the future."

Mrs. Reagan focused her "Just Say No" campaign on families and private-sector programs, refusing to align it with any government agency or to lobby for more federal drug-prevention funding. When she was criticized for failing to make full use of her political clout, she smiled and said, "A woman is like a tea bag: You don't know her strength until she's in hot water." ❦

Nancy Reagan scores, aided by Charles Barkley and Wayman Tisdale, at a "Just Say No" basketball game, February 4, 1988.

Oct. 17, 1989
Date

Dear Millie,
I want to ask you something.
Can you come to our school.
If you can come to our
school can you bring.
Mr. bush and mrs. bush

Your Friend,
Tasha

TASHA *to* MILLIE BUSH

Address Unknown · October 17, 1989

HARRY TRUMAN ONCE OFFERED ADVICE on dealing with criticism: "If you want a friend in Washington, get a dog." Truman wasn't much of a pet lover himself, but plenty of dogs have called 1600 Pennsylvania Avenue home. In addition to sharing the spotlight with their owners, many of them have achieved considerable fame in their own right: Franklin Roosevelt's Fala, for instance, got plenty of media coverage in his day and is prominently portrayed at the FDR Memorial in Washington. ❧Barbara Bush's springer spaniel Millie holds a

special distinction: She became the first White House dog to make the best-seller lists when *Millie's Book: As Dictated to Barbara Bush* was published in 1990. The book reportedly earned its canine co-author more in royalties than the President received in salary.

Even before she achieved literary fame, Millie was sufficiently well known to be the recipient of this letter from a kid named Tasha. Just before Halloween (obviously), when her teacher asked the class to write a letter to the White House, Tasha chose to invite Millie to visit her school in Virginia. Not wanting to appear rude, she tells Millie she can bring "Mr. Bush and Mrs. Bush" along if she wants to.

Millie died in 1997, having seen one of her puppies installed in the White House with George W. and Laura Bush. ❧

Former President Reagan left this sign in the patio outside the Oval Office to warn squirrels about Millie, the new occupant.

Mrs. George Bush
1600 Pennsylvania Avenue
Washington, DC 20500

29 January 1990

Dear Mrs Bush,

I surprise myself by feeling compelled to write you this note. It is my hope that it will ease concerns you may have regarding your husbands' February trip to South America.

My husband is the Special Agent-in-Charge of the DEA and has been assigned to our embassy in Bogota Colombia for the past two years.

Truely the only way I can deal with the nightmare of threats is by conciously choosing not to focus on the negatives. I am able to manage the stress because he loves what he does, believes in himself and the support he's given. He continually assures me that all

DEA Agent's Wife *to* Barbara Bush

Address Unknown · *January 29, 1990*

I F YOU'RE MARRIED TO A MAN WHO HAS A DANGEROUS JOB, you worry. Doesn't matter whether he's a fireman or a lion tamer or a soldier or a race car driver—if his work puts him in harm's way, you worry. For a woman in that position, dark fears and uncertainties are an inescapable fact of life, and nobody understands it better than another wife. That's what this letter is all about. ❧ Soon after the White House announced that the President would visit five nations in South America in 1990, First Lady Barbara Bush received this letter from a woman whose name and address have been

redacted for security reasons. As the wife of a Drug Enforcement Administration (DEA) agent assigned to Bogota, Colombia, the writer knows something about the occasional volatility of inter-American relations—and about what Mrs. Bush may be feeling.

"The only way I can deal with the nightmare of threats is by consciously choosing not to focus on the negatives," she writes. She knows her husband "loves what he does, believes in himself and the support he's given," and he assures her that "things will continue to be done cautiously *and* that right is on our side." There's nothing new or revelatory about the words, but they are especially meaningful because the nameless writer offers them "as one wife to another."

Fortunately, the trip to South America went off without a hitch, and President Bush returned home safe and sound. Other Chief Executives have not fared so well. Four have been murdered, and serious assassination attempts have endangered several others. Gerald Ford survived two attempts on his life in a single month in 1975, Ronald Reagan

was badly wounded in 1981, and Barbara Bush's husband was the target of a foiled car-bomb attack in Kuwait three years after this letter was written.

The casualty figures for DEA personnel are even higher. The DEA website lists scores of men and women who have died in the line of duty since 1921, among them two agents shot by suspected whiskey smugglers in Texas; another lost in a helicopter crash during a surveillance mission; a female agent killed with her unborn son in the explosion at the Murrah Federal Building in Oklahoma City; another, described as a man who "never asked a subordinate to undertake an assignment that he would not take on himself," shot during an undercover operation in Minnesota; and on and on and on. In 1976, an agent who apparently served in the same position as the husband of the woman who wrote this letter was murdered in his own office in Bogota.

The First Lady probably didn't have ready access to this information in 1990, and that's a good thing. It wouldn't have made her feel any better. ❧

THE SIMPSONS™

September 28, 1990

Mrs. Barbara Bush
The First Lady
The White House
1600 Pennsylvania Avenue
Washington, D.C.

Dear First Lady:

I recently read your criticism of my family.
I was deeply hurt. Heaven knows we're far
from perfect and, if truth be known, maybe
just a wee bit short of normal; but as Dr.
Seuss says, "a person is a person".

I try to teach my children Bart, Lisa, and
even little Maggie, always to give somebody
the benefit of the doubt and not talk badly
about them, even if they're rich. It's hard
to get them to understand this advice when
the very First Lady in the country calls us
not only dumb, but "the dumbest thing" she
ever saw. Ma'am, if we're the dumbest thing
you ever saw, Washington must be a good deal
different than what they teach me at the
current events group at the church.

I always believed in my heart that we had a
great deal in common. Each of us living our
lives to serve an exceptional man. I hope
there is some way out of this controversy. I
thought, perhaps, it would be a good start to
just speak my mind.

With great respect,

Marge Simpson

Marge Simpson

10201 West Pico Blvd., Los Angeles, California 90035   *Telephone:* 213.203.3993   *Fax* 213.203.3852

MARGE SIMPSON *to* BARBARA BUSH

Los Angeles, California • September 28, 1990

TELEVISION'S HIGHLY IRREVERENT ANIMATED SERIES *The Simpsons* debuted in the late 1980s and quickly became a popular favorite. By the end of the 1990s, the program had won a score of Emmy Awards, *Time* magazine had hailed it as the best TV show of all time, and ten-year-old hell-raiser Bart Simpson had been named one of the 100 most influential people of the 20th century. ❧ Barbara Bush was not a fan of the show. After she referred to it in a 1990 magazine interview as "the dumbest thing I've ever seen," she received this letter from Marge, the

much put-upon but indomitable matriarch of the Simpson clan. Admirably maintaining her dignity—no mean feat when you're sporting a three-foot-tall blue hairdo—Marge admits that her family may be "just a wee bit short of normal," but they still don't deserve a public smackdown from the First Lady. In fact,

Mrs. Simpson and Mrs. Bush have much in common: "Each of us [is] living our lives to serve an exceptional man."

An apologetic First Lady responded by thanking Marge for speaking her mind ("I foolishly didn't know you had one") and asking her to "forgive a loose tongue."

Sadly, this extremely civil exchange marked only a temporary cease-fire in the Bush Administration's feud with America's funniest dysfunctional family. In January 1992, President Bush told a gathering of the National Religious Broadcasters that his efforts to strengthen traditional values were intended to help American families become "a lot more like the Waltons and a lot less like the Simpsons." Naturally, that kind of attack could not go unanswered, and it didn't. In a subsequent episode of the show, the Simpsons were shown listening to the President's speech. When it ended, Bart exclaimed, "Hey, we're a lot like the Waltons. We're praying for the end of the depression, too."

The Bushes left the White House in 1993. *The Simpsons* is still going strong. ❧

Marge Simpson and Barbara Bush converse in The Simpsons *episode "Two Bad Neighbors."*

THE DALAI LAMA

October 30, 1995

Mrs. Hillary Rodham Clinton
The White House
Washington, DC 20500

Dear Mrs. Clinton,

I was very glad to have the opportunity to meet you, Chelsea and some of your friends and colleagues during my recent visit to Washington. It was a memorable evening. I particularly enjoyed learning about your trip to China and to Mongolia.

I felt that this trip to the United States was very productive and I was moved by the outpouring of support for the Tibetan people in the various cities I visited. While I was encouraged during this visit, I remain very concerned that the survival of the Tibetan civilization that thrived for centuries in Tibet is today threatened by repressive Chinese rule. With increased international pressure, however, I am hopeful that a positive change can be brought about in China's policies towards Tibet.

On behalf of the six million Tibetan people, I thank you for your interest and support for our cause.

With prayers and best wishes,

Yours sincerely,

Dalai Lama *to* Hillary Clinton

Address Unknown • *October 30, 1995*

WHO KNEW THAT HIS HOLINESS THE DALAI LAMA had a letterhead? ✽ Well, he does—and a nice one at that, with fanciful animals and strange writing on it, plus what may be mountain peaks at the top and a wheel-like mandala in the center. Here, the letterhead graces a thank-you letter that the Dalai Lama sent to First Lady Hillary Rodham Clinton in 1995. ✽ Most of us, particularly those who aren't First Lady of anything, will never receive a letter from a reincarnation of the Buddha, so a bit of biographical information is in order. He

was born Lhamo Dhondup in 1935 to a peasant family in a small village in Tibet. When he was barely three years old, he was visited by a high Tibetan official who had been directed to the boy's home by a vision. The official was wearing a rosary that had belonged to the recently deceased 13th Dalai Lama, and the boy recognized it and demanded that it be given to him.

After a series of tests convinced the official and his party of the child's true identity, he was proclaimed the 14th Dalai Lama, renamed Tenzin Gyatso, and shortly thereafter enthroned as Tibet's head of state. In 1959, a popular uprising demanded freedom from China, which had invaded Tibet a decade earlier. When the resistance movement collapsed, the Dalai Lama made a harrowing journey into exile in India, where he still lives.

Contrary to popular belief, the Dalai Lama is not the supreme spiritual authority for Buddhists, as the pope is for Roman Catholics. He is, however, a highly respected statesman and world traveler, the winner of the Nobel Peace Prize in 1989, the holder of a slot on *Time* magazine's list of the world's 100 most influential people,

a Presidential Distinguished Professor at Emory University in Georgia, the head of the Tibetan government in exile, and—by all accounts—an extremely charismatic, warm, and personable man.

In this letter, one of the world's best known men tells one of the world's best known women that he is glad to have met her during a visit to Washington. Then he moves to the issue that has been closest to his heart for many years: "I remain very concerned that the survival of the . . . civilization that thrived for centuries in Tibet is today threatened by repressive Chinese rule." He is encouraged, he writes, by the "outpouring of support for the Tibetan people" that he found in the United States, and he hopes that "increased international pressure" will bring about "positive change."

There is no indication that the "positive change" will come soon, but the Dalai Lama continues to advocate nonviolent opposition to Chinese rule in his homeland. It's the wise, gentle attitude to be expected from a man who once remarked, "Be kind whenever possible. It is always possible." ✽

EPPIE

December 5, '98.

Dear Hillary:

I saw you on C-Span this morning addressing the student body at Georgetown U. Your presentation on behalf of children was brilliant and moving.

Your ability at the podium is awesome. The applause and standing ovation let you know how much they appreciated your presentation. You had that audience in the palm of your hand.

I have no idea what your plans are after you leave the Whitehouse but of this I am certain — you can do anything you want — nothing is beyond your reach. Keep me posted.

Fondly,

Eppie

Eppie Lederer *to* Hillary Clinton

Address Unknown • *December 5, 1998*

L IFE AFTER THE WHITE HOUSE offers many challenges for a First Lady. Some relish the retreat to civilian life and the opportunity to reestablish "normal" relationships with friends and family away from the unceasing glare of the media spotlight. Others make the most of their prominence and newfound freedom by throwing themselves into causes that are important to them. Still others, particularly the many who find themselves widowed soon after leaving 1600 Pennsylvania Avenue, are dismayed to discover that life without the high-profile globetrotting and its

attendant "ruffles and flourishes" can be frustrating and lonely.

No one who knew First Lady Hillary Rodham Clinton expected her to fade into quiet retirement at the conclusion of her husband's second term as President, and she didn't. Early in 2000, long before the often tumultuous Clinton Administration ended, she announced her candidacy for the U.S. Senate. Several months later, the voters of America sent George W. Bush to the White House, and the voters of New York sent Hillary Rodham Clinton to the halls of Congress.

These history-making developments were still in the future when the First Lady received this brief note in 1998. The "Eppie" who wrote it was Esther Pauline Friedman Lederer, better known as Ann Landers. She and her identical twin sister, Pauline Esther Friedman Phillips, who used the pen name Abigail Van Buren, were the best known advice columnists of their day, dispensing witty, sometimes acerbic, no-nonsense doses of wisdom to millions of readers of their syndicated newspaper columns.

In this note, Landers, who had been a dinner guest at the White House on several occasions and had even spent a night in the Lincoln Bedroom in 1995, offers friendly words of commendation that must have been especially welcome at a time when the Judiciary Committee of the House of Representatives was considering several articles of impeachment against President Clinton. Completely ignoring the furor over the President's relationship with Monica Lewinsky, Landers begins by complimenting the First Lady on a recent "presentation on behalf of children" (Mrs. Clinton had a long-standing interest in the challenge of raising healthy children in modern society), then issues a warm and confident prediction: ". . . of this I am certain—you can do anything you want—nothing is beyond your reach."

In January 2007, Senator Clinton officially entered the race for the Presidency and quickly emerged as the front-runner. As of this writing, her nomination and election in 2008 are by no means assured, so it is not yet certain that she will fulfill Eppie's vision—but whether or not she wins this race, her groundbreaking post–White House career has already written a new chapter in First Lady history. &

THE WHITE HOUSE

September 12, 2001

Dear Children:

Many Americans were injured or lost their lives in the recent
national tragedy. All their friends and loved ones are feeling
very sad, and you may be feeling sad, frightened, or confused,
too.

I want to reassure you that many people - including your
family, your teachers, and your school counselor - love and
care about you and are looking out for your safety. You can
talk with them and ask them questions. You can also write
down your thoughts or draw a picture that shows how you are
feeling and share that with the adults in your life.

When sad or frightening things happen, all of us have an
opportunity to become better people by thinking about others.
We can show them we care about them by saying so and by
doing nice things for them. Helping others will make you feel
better, too.

I want you to know how much I care about all of you. Be kind
to each other, take care of each other, and show your love for
each other.

        With best wishes,

        Laura Bush

LAURA BUSH *to* CHILDREN

Washington, D.C. • September 12, 2001

AMERICANS AWOKE ON SEPTEMBER 11, 2001, to what promised to be a routine fall day, remarkable, if at all, for the brilliance of its sunshine and blue skies. By the time they went to bed that night, their world and their lives had changed. Hijacked planes had been flown into the towers of Manhattan's World Trade Center, sending two of America's tallest buildings crashing to the ground and murdering thousands. A third plane had smashed into the Pentagon, and wild rumors circulated that the Capitol and White House had been hit as

well. Yet another plane had plummeted to the ground in Pennsylvania after passengers rushed the hijackers and foiled their apparent plan to crash into a target in Washington.

For a while, no one knew where the attack had come from. As the full extent of the disaster became apparent, as rescue workers clawed through the rubble in New York and Virginia and Pennsylvania, as millions of viewers found themselves unable to tear their eyes away from the horrors that filled their television screens, feelings of shock and bewilderment were joined by waves of fear: Were more attacks coming, and if so, when and where?

Having worked as an elementary school teacher, First Lady Laura Bush knew that the burden of fright and helplessness was sure to weigh most heavily on the nation's young people. In response, she quickly drafted two letters—one to middle school and high school students, the other to children in the lower grades—and sent them to the superintendent of each state's department of education with a request that they be read in classrooms the following day.

Shown here is Mrs. Bush's message to elementary school children. It begins by assuring them that they shouldn't be ashamed of the unsettling welter of emotions they're experiencing: Lots of people, she writes, "are feeling very sad, and you may be feeling sad, frightened, or confused, too." She tells them not to keep their feelings bottled up, assuring them that the grown-ups around them "love and care about you and are looking out for your safety" and suggesting that they ask questions about what's happened, or maybe even draw a picture "that shows how you are feeling." After urging the children to reach out to those around them—"Helping others will make you feel better, too"—the letter closes with the written equivalent of a big, warm hug: "I want you to know how much I care about all of you."

No previous First Lady had taken on a role quite like this one. With a simple message of reassurance—she says, in effect, that a bad thing has happened, but it'll be all right soon—the President's wife became, at least temporarily, a surrogate mother for some of the nation's youngest and most vulnerable citizens. ❧

Deborah Butryn
Lakeside School
Oak Street
Manistique, Michigan 49854

March 12, 2003

Mrs. Laura Bush
The White House
1600 Pennsylvania Avenue
Washington ,D.C.

Dear Mrs. Bush:

I teach kindergarten in Manistique, a small rural community in Michigan's Upper Peninsula. In keeping with Presidents' Day, I hung a poster of all of the United States Presidents in my room. I found that my students showed a very keen interest in the Presidents and were asking many questions about them and their families. I had a copy of the September, 2002, issue of <u>Biography</u> magazine which featured a great article on America's First Ladies and I shared it with my class. They were fascinated to learn that President Bush had such a pretty wife and were absolutely amazed that he actually had a mother! I told them that you had been an elementary school teacher and one of my students suggested that we write to you! I thought you might be amused by some of the responses to the question that I posed to them: "What do you think Mrs. Bush does during her busy day?"

Shelbey: "She has to help him with all of his paperwork and then she helps him clean up his office.   She takes care of him when he is sick and puts cold cloths on his head.

Todd: " She goes to a lot of meetings and she wears pretty suits. She, also, has to shovel the snow and feed the birds".

Chester: " She sweeps the floor and cooks carrots and vegetable soup".

Megan: " She feeds the dog and cooks carrot soup for dinner. She plants the daffodils and she does the President's speeches when he isn't feeling well".

Dylan:" She picks out the shirts and ties for the President".

DEBORAH BUTRYN *to* LAURA BUSH

Manistique, Michigan • March 12, 2003

W E END OUR RUMMAGE through 200 years' worth of the First Ladies' mail just as we began it, with a question: What does a First Lady really do? ❧ People have pondered the question ever since Martha Washington's day, but most of us still have trouble answering it with any precision. Imagine how profoundly a child must be stumped by it. Many kids are aware that the First Lady lives in the White House (*cool!*), so they imagine she spends lots of time having kings and queens and movie stars over for fancy dinners. On the other hand, those who know that she is

somebody's wife and somebody's mother (*boy, are her kids lucky!*) realize that she may get saddled with many of the chores and problems that their own moms have to deal with. It's confusing.

Some of that confusion is evident in this letter from a kindergarten teacher in Michigan. To mark Presidents' Day in 2003, Deborah Butryn showed her students some pictures of the Presidents and First Ladies. "They were fascinated to learn that President Bush had such a pretty wife," she reports, and when she asked them, "What do you think Mrs. Bush does during her busy day?" they gave her an earful.

Several see the First Lady primarily as a housewife: "She sweeps the floor and cooks carrots and vegetable soup," writes one, and another adds that she has to "do a lot of vacuuming." Two students are especially worried about the challenge of caring for the White House vases—and rightly so, since any kid knows that vases are fragile things, and if you drop one and break it, you're in Big Trouble.

Shelbey and Dylan cast her in the role of helpmate: She assists the President with

his paperwork, picks out his shirts and ties, and "puts cold cloths on his head" when he's sick. Finally, Megan and Todd identify her as a competent, successful woman of the world who is perfectly capable of filling in for the President on a speaking tour, "goes to a lot of meetings" and "wears pretty suits."

The thing is, most of the answers are absolutely correct—except maybe the one about shoveling the snow off the White House driveway.

Question: What does a First Lady really do? *Answer*: Everything.

It may seem simplistic, even flippant, but it's not far from the truth: She does it all, or at least she's expected to try. Woman, daughter, wife, mother, helpmate, cheerleader, standard-bearer, teacher, advocate, listener, diplomat, hostess, lightning rod, speechmaker, comforter, challenger, even symbol of America—she has to be all of them, sequentially and simultaneously, all the time. It's what makes the job of being First Lady an opportunity, a burden, a joy.

The good news is that she really doesn't have to wash all those vases. ❧

Transcriptions

Of Selected Letters

The following section provides transcriptions of selected letters that appear within the body of the book. The original spelling and capitalization have been retained.

page 28

Thomas Jefferson to Abigail Adams

Dear Madam,

The affectionate sentiments which you have had the goodness to express in your letter of May 20, towards my dear departed daughter, have awakened in me sensibilities natural to the occasion, & recalled your kindnesses to her, which I shall ever remember with gratitude & friendship. I can assure you with truth, they had made an indelible impression on her mind, and that to the last, on our meetings after long separations, whether I had heard lately of you, and how you did, were among the earliest of her inquiries. In giving you this assurance I perform a sacred duty for her, & at the same time, am thankful for the occasion furnished me, of expressing my regret that circumstances should have arisen, which have seemed to draw a line of separation between us. The friendship with which you honored me has ever been valued, and fully reciprocated; & altho' events have been passing which might be trying to some minds, I never believed yours to be of that kind, nor felt that my own was. Neither my estimate of your character, nor the esteem founded in that, have ever been lessened for a single moment, although doubts whether it would be acceptable may have forbidden manifestations of it.

Mr. Adams's friendship & mine began at an earlier date. It accompanied us thro' long & important scenes. The different conclusions we had drawn from our political reading & reflections, were not permitted to lessen mutual esteem; each party being conscious they were the result of an honest conviction in the other. Like differences of opinion existing among our fellow citizens, attached them to one or the other of us, and produced a rivalship in their minds which did not exist in ours. We never stood in one another's way; for if either had been withdrawn at any time, his favorers would not have gone over to the other, but would have sought for some one of homogeneous opinions. This consideration was sufficient to keep down all jealousy between us, & to guard our friendship from any disturbance by sentiments of rivalship; and I can say with truth, that one act of Mr. Adams's life, and one only, ever gave me a moment's personal displeasure. I did consider his last appointments to office as personally unkind. They were from among my most ardent political enemies, from whom no faithful co-operation could ever be expected; and laid me under the embarrassment of acting thro' men whose views were to defeat mine, or to encounter the odium of putting others in their places. It seemed but common justice to leave a successor free to act by instruments of his own choice. If my respect for him did not permit me to ascribe the whole blame to the influence of others, it left something for friendship to forgive, and after brooding over it for some little time, and not always resisting the expression of it, I forgave it cordially, and returned to the same state of esteem & respect for him which had so long subsisted. Having come into life a little later than Mr. Adams, his career has preceded mine, as mine is followed by some other; and it will probably be closed at the same distance after him which time originally placed between us. I maintain for him, & shall carry into private life, an uniform & high measure of respect and good will and for yourself a sincere attachment.

I have thus, my dear Madam, opened myself to you without reserve, which I have long wished an opportunity of doing; and without knowing how it will be received, I feel relief from being unbosomed. And I have now only to entreat your forgiveness for this transition from a subject of domestic affliction,

to one which seems of a different aspect. But tho'
connected with political events, it has been viewed
by me most strongly in it's unfortunate bearings
on my private friendships. The injury these have
sustained has been a heavy price for what has never
given me equal pleasure. That you may both be
favored with health, tranquillity and long life, is the
prayer of one who tenders you the assurance of his
highest consideration and esteem.

∽⊘∼

Tuesday, Augt. 23d 1814
Dear Sister,
My husband left me yesterday morng. to join Gen.
Winder. He enquired anxiously whether I had
courage, or firmness to remain in the President's
house until his return, on the morrow, or
succeeding day, and on my assurance that I had no
fear but for him and the success of our army, he left
me, beseeching me to take care of myself, and of the
cabinet papers, public and private. I have since recd.
two despatches from him, written with a pencil; the
last is alarming, because he desires I should be ready
at a moment's warning to enter my carriage and
leave the city; that the enemy seemed stronger than
had been reported, and that it might happen that
they would reach the city, with intention to destroy
it. . . . I am accordingly ready; I have pressed as many
cabinet papers into trunks as to fill one carriage;
our private property must be sacrificed, as it is
impossible to procure wagons for its transportation.
I am determined not to go myself until I see Mr
Madison safe, and he can accompany me, as I hear
of much hostility towards him, ... disaffection
stalks around us. . . . My friends and acquaintances
are all gone; Even Col. C with his hundred men,
who were stationed as a guard in the enclosure. . . .
French John (a faithful domestic,) with his usual
activity and resolution, offers to spike the cannon
at the gate, and to lay a train of powder which would
blow up the British, should they enter the house.
To the last proposition I positively object, without
being able, however, to make him understand why
all advantages in war may not be taken.

Wednesday morning, twelve o'clock. Since sunrise
I have been turning my spyglass in every direction
and watching with unwearied anxiety, hoping to
discern the approach of my dear husband and his
friends, but, alas, I can descry only groups of military
wandering in all directions, as if there was a lack of
arms, or of spirit to fight for their own firesides!

Three O'clock. Will you believe it, my Sister?
We have had a battle or skirmish near Bladensburg,
and I am still here within sound of the cannon! Mr.
Madison comes not; may God protect him! Two
messengers covered with dust, come to bid me fly;
but I wait for him. . . . At this late hour a wagon has
been procured, I have had it filled with the plate
and most valuable portable articles belonging to
the house; whether it will reach its destination; the
Bank of Maryland, or fall into the hands of British
soldiery, events must determine.

Our kind friend, Mr. Carroll, has come to hasten
my departure, and is in a very bad humor with me
because I insist on waiting until the large picture of
Gen. Washington is secured, and it requires to be
unscrewed from the wall. This process was found
too tedious for these perilous moments; I have
ordered the frame to be broken, and the canvass
taken out it is done, and the precious portrait placed
in the hands of two gentlemen of New York, for
safe keeping. And now, dear sister, I must leave
this house, or the retreating army will make me a
prisoner in it, by filling up the road I am directed to
take. When I shall again write you, or where I shall
be tomorrow, I cannot tell!!

∽⊘∼

Lady will thou permit the dark browned Son of the
of a Chippewa to address his petition to thee he is
told thou could speak in the ears of thine Uncle the
President and that he will {illegible} to what thou
sayest. Years ago, I left my forest home to be relocated
among the good White People. Last Summer when
the leaves were green and the flowers were in bloom
I though I would go and visit my people; after
journeying many ways my heart was again gladdened
with the sight of the woody groves and silvery waters

where the wigwams of my father had once stood. But now alas, all was silent and and desolate: only the numerous Graves that dotted the hillside told the fate of my once numerous kindred. The Whiskey Demon; had been there, and with his poisonous breath he had slain my people as a Destroying Angel he had made desolate the once quiet and happy homes of the simple children of nature too well I understood the course; for when the wise drum of our nations were gathered in council, they declared that our Great Father, the Resident and his sages had enacted wise and just laws in our behalf; but that the men that had been sent among us to enforce those laws had been with one {illegible} exceptions had unprincipled {illegible}; whose whole aim was to rob us once {illegible} themselves now we do not think that our Great-Father, the President is aware of the true state of these things; but we think that we have been misrepresented, and that the Great Freebooter—Rice M. C. has chasened the ears of the President while his friends were plundering us to the end that our Father might not hear the cries for {illegible} of his red Children; our present Agent is a great Drunkard he is also a very selfish; profane and wicked man; and through the Secret intrigueings and machinations of his Rumsellers; he has instigated the Indians to drive the Good Missionaries from among us; and with them has gone our only future hope of being reclaimed and ranked among Christian nations; under the patronage of the Rev. Dr. Breck DD a Good work was begun among us, and the Indians were rapidly embracing Christianity and were also beginning to till the soil with much {illegible} and advantage to themselves. But the whiskey traders foresaw that if the light of truth prevailed that the hop of their Gain would be gone; so the used all their deceptive arts to induce the ignorant and {illegible} among us to drive that Good man away and now my people are left to be deceived by these men who prey upon their fellows, to perish in their ignorance with no messengers of Jesus, to point out the way of the Whiteman's Heaven. The undergrowth of ages has hidden the right way that leads to happy hunting grounds, the pleasant path that leads to the spirit Land and is {illegible}; Must I journey alone to the {illegible} of Jesus alone; must I light the watchfires of my nation upon the hills of Paradise. In Solitude shall I listen to the Sweet music of Heaven; Shall none of my people go with me; Oh when will the wise and good men of your nation lend us a helping hand to drive out these Locusts of Egypt from among us, when will they send us good men to kindle a beacon of hope in the Temple of truth. That even the poor Redmen may discern the paths of wisdom and now oh Lady I entreat you. Speak for my people. Tell your Friends to counsel our White Father to remove our Agent and to appoint—a God fearing and truth loving man in his Stead tell him to do so in haste before the dark wores of oblivion corer us and hides his red children forever from his view, we fear not the Bottle {illegible} of the fierce Docotah; nor the glittering pointed steel of the pale faced warriors of you nation. But oh we fear {illegible} that justly that whiskey and its killing influence will blot out forever the records of our existence. Whiskey is plentiful as water here among us and at this time no efforts are made by those in authority to stay its progress; Those delegations of our people that visit the Capitol to ask for money are always influenced to do so by the {illegible} is made use of to extort money from the Government to enrich those corteous men, money is a curse to the Indians as they only use it to secure whiskey and it has a tendency to induce {illegible} and Robbers to come among us implements of husbandry is what we need and Good faithful men as teachers and General advisors if you point out these things we know that our white father sees for us the Eagle in his loftiest flight and we trust that he will stretch forth his hands to Save his Red Children I have journeyed for from the wigwams and have spoken for myself. But my purse is getting light So I have concluded to return from whence I came and thus have I forwarded my communications trusting that they will Reach their destination.

⁂

page 38:
HELEN M. RAUSCHNABEL TO MARY TODD LINCOLN

Rochester May 7th 1861
Mrs. Lincoln,
Dear Lady please excuse the freedom I take of addressing a few lines to you I am an American Girl, my parents were born in the State of Vermont, but I was born in the City of Troy N Y. I have been

employed for a few years back, writing the mail, for the Independent, at the Independent office Number 5 Beckman St New York City while in this City I became acquainted with a German whom I married May 10 1860 only one year ago, He belongs to that class of sober honest industrious Germans who are so consciously striving to beautify and in rich our beloved Country, he is a great admirer of Mr Lincoln, and is ready to give up his life for the defence of his adopted Country he seems to despise the effeminacy of our American people, who are fleeing into Canada to escape from the war, now in these perilous times when their efforts are most needed.

At the time of election his heart was all for Mr Lincoln and the republican party, but could not vote because his papers had not been issued long enough but many were the controversies he had with his German friends to get them to enlist in the right cause.

Dear Lady my object in writing this letter to you was not to give you the history of my life, or to proclaim the merits of my husband, altho what I have already written may seem so. It was merely to relate a remarkable dream I had last night about Mr Lincoln which I think has a significant meaning, & I thought perhaps it might be a comfort to you in these perilous times.

I dreamed it stormed & thundered & lightned terribly, it seemed as tho the Heavens & Earth were coming together, but it soon ceased, still there seemed to be very dark clouds sailing thro the horizon, I thought I stood pensively viewing the scene, when a man resembling Mr Lincoln appeared standing erect in the firmament with a book in his hand, he stood as near as I could calculate over the City of Washington, his head seemed reared above the lightnings flash and thunder bolt, the sun seemed to be just rising in the East, and its rays shed a soft mellow light around about him, beneath his feet rolled dark & heavy clouds which the sun light was fast dispelling, I saw him walk thro all the Southern part of the horizon with a book in one hand, & a pen in the other when he got to the western part of the firmament he made a halt & stood erect, he was crowned with honors & covered with Laurels, and looked very smiling. I thought I clapped my hands & sung the following verse which I well remembered when I awoke & arose from my bed & penned it to paper

A voice from the North has proclaimed the glad Morn
And Slavery is ended & Freedom is born
The fair Sunny South is restor'd one more
Secession is ended & Slavery is ore.

Mrs President Lincoln, if you could find it in your heart to write to one so humble, just a few lines in answer to this, I should cherish all thro life as one of my choicest relics.

∽

PAGE 46:

QUEEN VICTORIA TO MARY TODD LINCOLN

Osborne.
April 29—1865.
Dear Madam,
Though a stranger to you I cannot remain silent when so terrible a calamity has fallen upon you & your country, & most personally express my deep & heartfelt sympathy with you under the shocking circumstances of your present dreadful misfortunes.

No one can better appreciate than I can, who am myself utterly broken-hearted by the loss of my own beloved Husband, who was the Light of my Life,—my Stay—my All,—What your sufferings must be; and I earnestly pray that you may be supported by Him to whom alone the sorely stricken can look for comfort, in this hour of heavy affliction.

With the renewed expression of true sympathy, I remain, dear Madam, Your Sincere friend.

∽

page 52:
MRS. E. C. SLOAN TO LUCRETIA GARFIELD

Baltimore March 8th 1881
Mrs. Garfield,
Hon. of Respected Madam
I come in behalf of suffering humanity to beg that you will attain to the high honor of your predecessor, The Hon. Mrs. Hayes whose fame will resound to the end of time for her firmness to "Duty" in opposition to {illegible} in banishing the "Intoxicating {illegible}" from the "White House". Be firm, be strong, and God will help you along.

There is no safety—only in Total Abstinence and its progress must be onward for God is so ordaining" and the will come when "Woman" will exterminate Rum, the cause of so much suffering in almost any household. The rich the poor, the learned and the unlearned all fall victims to the accursed Poison, a little more time a little more rum and those you see and love may soon succumb; its effects are ever the same. God help you to adapt and remain firm to the principals of "Total Abstinence" for only on that rock man and woman can stand without tottering in every grade of society—we see the evidence.

P.S. Please let me know your views in regard to Woman Suffrage as that will be the next-needed reform for the perpetuity of good government—from husband's own account danger stares us in the face. The ballot being controlled by such a "Map" of illiterate and ignorant men. The intelligent American Woman has more a right in the interest of her country than an incompetent and illiterate foreigner—and she a tax payer deprived of the right of Representation—{illegible} in the highest sense.

✑

page 58:
HOWARD CARTER TO CAROLINE HARRISON

Lennox Park
Dorsey, Howard Co, Md
Mrs. Harrison
Dear Madame
I am very sorry you are sick and send you a bird and {illegible} tomatoes hoping you will enjoy them when you know that I shot the bird for you hoping it will do you as much good as some birds I shot for a sick lady. Last Fall the Doctor said she could not live but she enjoyed the bird and is still living. I would shoot you some partridge but our law is not up yet and mama says we must obey the laws of our state as well as Gods laws so I send you the best I could get and promise you some partridges when I can shoot them hoping you will accept my little present and that our Heavenly Father will restore your health and that I shall have the pleasure of seeing you some day as I have not been to Washington. With best wishes I am most sincerely your little friend.

✑

page 64:
FRANCES CLEVELAND TO H. T. THURBER

11 July 94
Gray Gables
Buzzards Bay Mass
Dear Mr. Thurber,
I don't want by any chance to have a word of this get to the President because he is worried and anxious enough but I want to ask your advice and assistance. We have of course had no kind of watchman of any kind here. And we have been absolutely without fear, but yesterday Wm Brad discovered three different very tough looking men on different parts of the place. They all seemed to go away about noon & just at evening one of them was found again.

Brad put him off & had quite a time Wm. Told me and we at once had Mr. Briggs the {illegible} of the town informed & he brought a watchman. Who staid all night & has returned tonight & a constable has watched all day. They have had a town meeting today & sworn Brad in as a special constable. They are all worried & anxious & think the men are after the children. Of course it troubles me considerably & it is such a lonely sort of place. I have wondered if you might deem it best to have a secret service man or Detective sent on to help these local people out. I don't want to be silly, but the times are to queer & every thing seems so uncertain that it looks to be only right to take every precaution even to the extent of going too far. I shouldn't like to do anything to hurt the feeling of the local authorities because they are most interested & kind & excited but it might if you thought it best be done in a way of helping them out as being quite a strain on them. I know you are as over-cautious as I am. There are never toughs or tramps in this vicinity it is entirely a new thing. For myself, I shouldn't worry—but the children—that is another matter. Please let me know what you think wise.

I hope you are well, the poor President is under a fearful strain and responsibility. I won't send my love to him. I would rather he did not know of my writing.

✑

June 1, 1906.
Alma Tadema, the artist, told me the other evening a little story about Winston Churchill's encounter with one of his brother artists which may interest you. As Tadema told it, the artist was making a little sketch of a group of noted people gathered at some social occasion. The sketch was intended for publication and Winston was not one of those to be included. He thought it a good group to be in, however, and kept hovering about it and putting himself under the artist's eye until the latter rather in self defence sketched him in slightly in profile in the outer line.

When the sketch was finished they were all crowding around to look at it and expressing, as is apt to be the case at such times, favorable opinions of the artist's work. Winston, having got into the picture in this fashion, came up to give his opinion and in his characteristic way said: "I don't agree with you. I don't think the likenesses are good at all. Look at that thing of me. Surely that isn't like me." The artist, whom Tadema described as one of the most patient and gentle-spoken of his race, turned at this like the proverbial worm. "Yes," he said, "I think you are right, Mr. Churchill. It doesn't do you full justice, but then you see it is in profile, so that I could only get in half your cheek."

Any little story like this against Winston is received with delight in London. There is nobody at the moment more thoroughly unpopular, in fact, detested in the more important social circles. They don't like him as a Liberal, and they don't respect him as a "turn coat"; but for his bad manners, his recklessness and the row he has stirred up in South Africa, they hate him. Last night we were dining with the Princess Christian, the sister of the King. In some way Winston's name was mentioned, and she turned to me, saying in a semi-confidential whisper: "I musn't say it publicly, but I detest him." About the same time on the opposite side of the table, as I learned afterward, Prince Christian was saying to Mrs. Reid: "I don't dare to say what I think of that young man. If I spoke my mind I should be in danger of being as violent as he is himself."

At the moment, this boy is one of the most prominent people in the House of Commons, and scarcely one of the older members shows much more ability in catching the ear of the House or in making what might be called distinctly "smart" speeches. His fertility, too, is wonderful. While the Natal business was uppermost, he was badgered by questions every day to which he generally made uncommonly effective replies, and he was making set speeches every few days. Since then he has made two or three rather important public addresses. During the vile weather in the second and third weeks of May he was laid up with a dangerous influenza, but the very day he got back somewhat convalescent from Blenheim he spoke in the House and made the speech of the evening at the big Australian dinner.

Still his health is undoubtedly bad, and people on both sides say he is burning the candle at both ends, and is likely to go the way his father did. { . . . }

As you may have noticed, a vast deal of the gossip I hear about public men is set afloat by the wives of other public men at the dinner tables. A rather startling bit of it came to me the other night from a Conservative lady, who declared that of late Mr. Asquith, under the burdens of office, dissensions in the Cabinet, annoyance at C.-B.'s slowness in getting out of the way by going to the House of Lords, etc., had taken to drink. If the story is true, I don't believe anybody outside has yet got much idea of it. He doesn't look like tat sort of man, hasn't acted that way when I have met him at public dinners—and, in short, I don't believe it. { . . . }

I cannot guess in the least whether the little particulars above, about such things as the Princess Christian's dinner, interest you at all. If they do not, you had better skip what remains of this letter. For it has occurred to me to put down some of the details of a Court and a Levee, on the mere chance of your caring to read somewhat minutely concerning things you have known about in general all your life.

I think I told you once about how a Levee went at Buckingham Palace. They have been held of late at St. James', and the public like this better, because it makes a fine show for them, when the King and Court come in State procession from Buckingham Palace to St. James's. The King times his departure so as to arrive at St. James's at exactly twelve. He is escorted by the Horse Guards and accompanied by a member of the Royal Princes and the great officers of the Household. The procession generally consists of from four to six State carriages, with two men in the Royal livery seated on the box and two men standing on the footboard behind. The King's carriage has four horses. The bands play as they drive into the courtyard at St. James's nearest the throne room, and a moment or two later, the Ambassadors, who are apt to be either in the room immediately beyond it or in the one to the side of it, can see the King, preceded by two officers of the Court walking backwards with their wands of office in their hands, approaching the throne and taking his seat. The Royal Princes stand on either side of him, and a line of the great officers of the Court stretches down to the door through which everybody is to enter. The throne is simply a hug gilt chair, with a crown worked in the back of the upholstering and another in the top of the gilt work at the back, and it stands on a slightly elevated dais under the big Royal canopy, where again the decoration of the crown is to be seen in one or two places. The King sits well forward in the chair, ready to rise when the Ambassadors come in, and with a heavy velvet cushion on the floor in front for a footstool, which he used while he was lame, but hasn't used for the late Levees. The band in the courtyard was playing when he took his seat on the throne, and it begins again the moment the Lord Chamberlain gives the signal for the Ambassadors to enter. Then all goes as at Buckingham Palace.

Now for a Court. This is a much more serious thing, and as there is one to-night, I have just been explaining to our representative at The Hague, Dr. David Jayne Hill, precisely how he is to enter, when he is to make his bows, and where he is to take his place to watch the rest of the proceedings. The mise en scene is much the same, excepting that the room at Buckingham Palace is rather larger. The lane is formed in the same way between the Royalties on the left of the dais and the men-at-arms. The Queen sits at the left of the King; and immediately behind are the Mistress of Robes and some of the Ladies-in-Waiting, while in the same line, but on lower seats, are the Princess of Wales and any of the other Princesses who may be present. The Princes are at the King's right and rather behind the officers of the Court who pass up the cards.

The diplomatic corps are received in two rooms by themselves, the men in one, the ladies in the other. The fact that the King and Queen have taken their places is known by a rather low flourish of trumpets, and the line advances at once, with the wife of the Russian Ambassador, who is the doyenne of the corps (Cambon having no wife). She is followed by the ladies of her Embassy, and by any ladies she is to present. After making her deep courtesys, first to the King and then to the Queen, she steps a little towards them and makes a half turn to present each of her Embassy and any others she presents as they advance. Then she bows again and retires, taking her place at the end of the first cross bench, in a line with the throne but facing it. The other Ambassadresses follow in the same way, then the wives of the Ministers. The moment the ladies of the diplomatic corps have finished France advances at the head of the line of Ambassadors, and each in turn goes through the same thing, the only difference between this and the Levee being that there are two profound bows in place of one, with a step or two forward after the first to bring you in front of the Queen for the second. During the Court the King and Queen remain seated all the time not shaking hands with anybody.

Some of the ladies manage their trains with great skill and grace, and the sight is really beautiful. Others appear to be weighed down and pulled back by them, some in danger of tripping on them, and altogether have trouble, from which one of the officers, the moment they get through the line relieves them by grasping the train, folding it up and flinging it across the ladies arm. Others, and particularly the stout and ambitious ones, have no end of trouble about their courtesys. At the last Court one substantial English matron sank so near the floor that we thought she was going to sit on it, and then came a moment of awful agony for her and suspense for the onlookers when it was a question whether her muscular powers were sufficient to bring her up again. Her eyes rolled, her face assumed a die-away expression, but at last she got up, to the relief of everybody. Even the sad faced Queen was detected in a surreptitious and fleeting smile as the stout party passed out of sight. Others are so frightened as to be almost rigid and scarcely make any courtesy at all. It must be admitted the most of them do it gracefully; and certainly at the last Court non more gracefully than our American line, which included among others the pretty debutante daughter of Mr. and Mrs. Carter.

This sort of thing goes on for an hour and a half. It as quite midnight when the King and Queen rose, made their bows and filed out towards the supper room. { . . . }

In a much more agreeable way we are crowded almost constantly on the subject of admissions to Parliament. There is no chance of admitting ladies at all to the House of Commons, since no tickets are issued to us for them, and the only way they can get in is through the favor of some member of the House, who gives them his wife's or his daughter's ticket. As there are only thirty or forty of these each day for a membership of over six hundred, and as the members are very keen for them themselves, the Embassy never asks for them, though in special cases it is sometimes possible to get a hint to a member which leads to his offer of a ticket.

Half the politicians who come ask casually and as a matter of course for tickets for a party of six or eight, including their wives and daughters, and are not only amazed, but sometimes outraged, by the misconduct of the British Government, when they find that only two tickets are issued to us each day and that is double the number issued to any other Embassy. They promptly express their opinion of the outrage the Government is guilty of in not enlarging the House of Commons sufficiently to provide galleries for their accommodation! These are some of the humors of the service—though truth to tell some of our compatriots don't take a humorous view of it at all!

And here an end.

∾❧⁓

page 78:
MRS. PINCUS SCHEIN TO HELEN TAFT

113 Ridge St. N. Y. City
March 9, 1910
Dear Madam,
I address this letter to you because all else has failed. I have a son, Solomon Schein, eleven years old, who, until recently was in Europe with my father. Now, my father died and my child was left alone without anyone to take care of him.

My husband, a citizen of the United States, brought him to this country from Europe, but the immigration officials at Ellis Island refuse to admit

him. (the child) claiming he is an idiot though merely badly tongue-tied.

Dear Madam, you too, are a mother and can feel with me. I, therefore, appeal to you. For, if my child is deported, no nation will accept him as my husband has severed all connections by becoming a citizen. There is nobody who will take care of him and he will be left alone, an outcast without the guidance of any friend.

My husband, my children, and I are willing to work and do everything possible towards maintaining my child, if we but get permission.

A favorable reply from you will assuage a stricken mother. This child, who has borne more than is allotted to one of his age, will be ever grateful for your service in delivering him from solitary desertion among a mass of strangers.

I remain, a mother in suspense and anguish.

Yours with thanks,

P. S. The child is to be deported on Saturday, the 12th of March in the morning. Please do not delay your message of hope and grant him admission in view of extenuating circumstances.

∾❧⁓

page 79:
MRS. PINCUS SCHEIN TO HELEN TAFT

March 15, 1910
My dear Mr. President,
I beg to return the letter from Mrs. Pincus Schein. We have concluded to direct the admission of the boy. The case is one of unusual hardship, and the family has Mrs. Taft to thank for the decision. Stripped of {illegible} I am sure our decision is right.

∾❧⁓

page 80:
HELEN TAFT TO MME. YUKIO OZAKI

My dear Mme. Ozaki
I received your very interesting letter describing how the cherry trees came to Washington. And I am delighted to hear this. My remarks were

responsible for the beautiful gift {illegible}. I planted fifty the first year and fifty the next year—in the other part of the park, so I thought it was that planting {illegible} made the Mayor of Tokio send them {illegible} and I am delighted to hear the truth at last.

I am very sorry to hear of your illness and hope you are getting well now. I am so glad that you and your husband are coming to Washington later. I will be with warmest embraces in Washington the middle of October making visit, before {illegible}.

With sincere gratitude for letting me know the true history of the cherry trees and with warmest regards—

∾◊◞

page 96:

THE WOMEN'S LEAGUE OF MIAMI FLORIDA
TO LOU HOOVER

El Comodoro Hotel
Miami Florida
June 18—1929
Mrs. H. Hoover,
Washington D. C.,
You remember that Florida, Va., North Carolina, Tenn. & Texas {illegible} Mr. Hoover, a large majority last fall. Well "We" thought we were putting a "real" White "Lady" in the White House. Didn't even dream that you would disgrace the White House by associating with Negroes.

We ("The Southern States") are very very much disappointed in you. We thought you were a real lady. You having {illegible} Negro women in the White House will cause Mr. Hoover to loose several million votes all the Southern States if he wants to run again. Also we are loosing confidence in him any way we thought he was for the people. But he has turned his back to the people that elected him and put himself in the hands of the interests. And is for the privileged few.

You can go to Illinois next winter and visit your Negro friend.

FLORIDA
Don't care for you to visit the South anymore.

The Women's League of Miami Fla.

∾◊◞

page 112:

CLARA LEONARD TO ELEANOR ROOSEVELT

Miami, Fla.
Dec. 14, 1934
Dear Madame—
I am a widow with a son fourteen years of age and am trying to support him and myself and keep him in school on a very small sum which I make.

I feel worthy of asking you about this: I am greatly in need of a coat. If you have one which you have laid aside from last season would appreciate it so much if you would send it to me. I will pay postage if you see fit to send it. I wear size 36 or 38. { . . . }

I assure you I am worthy of any help you render.

∾◊◞

page 120:

PVT. CLIFTON SEARLES TO ELEANOR ROOSEVELT

Pvt. Clifton Searles
E.R.G. Unasigned U.S. Army
13,178,798
c/o Lincoln University
Lincoln University Park
Box 209
Jan 11th 1942 {sic}
8:25
Mrs. Roosevelt:
While visiting your city and the headquarters of the nation I had a most interesting thing to happen.

I stopped at the People's Drug Store, 7th & M. Street N.W. and asked for a small soda. The clerk called to another clerk, one coke to take out. My instant reply was I don't want to take it out, I should like to drink it here. I was served in a paper cup, while a white man beside me was served in a glass. Asking why the paper cup, I was told it was the policy of the store.

Please note, I'm expected to be call to active service very soon, I have a lot to fight for so the white man says. My four brothers are in the service, but as to what they are fighting for God only knows.

I'm going to feel fine, fighting in a Jim Crow army, for a Jim Crow government. Joe Louis once said "we are on God's side. Yes it might be true, but God never captain a Jim Crow army, nor does he reach down and give Negro soldier's a drink of water in a paper cup.

Yes I'm going to fight, but I'll be fighting for my race, for my people and when I might see a white boy lying on a battle field, I hope to God I won't remember People's Drug Store on Jan. 11th.

I realize you are for the common man, and your husband also but for the other people (white). Hitler and the Japs could win the war if it meant giving the Negro equality.

Oh! Yes, I noticed that on the radio, they use the term "yellow japs," I think that China have yellow skinned people. Maybe I'm wrong. This is just to let you know how one negro soldier feel going into the service.

P. S. Here's the cup, to bad some negro boy couldn't give a dying boy (white) a cooling drink on a battle field. God bless the white man, and teach him something about brotherhood & Democracy.

∞

page 126:
LORENA HICKOK TO ELEANOR ROOSEVELT

Friday
April 13th 1945
Dearest:

It seems like only a few minutes ago when I was writing you, yesterday, a long letter about housekeeping and gardening and feeling, although I did not mention it, very complacent about the progress of the war and the outcome of the S.F. conference. I guess I never realized what implicit faith I had in him until now since he has gone.

I still think, God help me, that Truman will make a better President right now than Henry would have made. At least, at the business of getting along with Congress. But I also have an uneasy wondering if he will get along with Congress by letting Congress run him. Also, I don't like his closeness to Hannegan. You will infer and your inference will be correct that I haven't much use for Mr. Hannegan. One thing I think I never fully appreciated before was that one never had to worry about the President letting anybody run him.

Dear, last night I wrote you a pretty dazed and incoherent letter, which I am tearing up. It was wonderful and reassuring to hear your voice this morning. No use burdening you with my bewilderment and terror. After all, I guess I only felt like millions of other people in the word. And they'll all be telling you! You are like that—people are instinctively drawn to you for comfort, even when you are in trouble yourself. And I guess I'm like all the rest.

For you and your future I have no worries at all—although I do hope you will take at least a few weeks off this Spring and Summer to rest. You will find your place a very active and important place, I feel sure—and fill it superbly. I'd like to hope that it may be something in which I can help you if only indirectly, from the sidelines in a way. You know, you are going to be more your own agenda, freer to act, that you've ever been before. Only, for goodness' sake, do take care of yourself and keep strong and well. We've seen one magnificent constitution break and go down under overwork and strain. God, he used to be so strong, so vital, so full of energy! I'm glad I didn't see much of him these last few years. I'd rather remember him as I knew him and saw him so often in the thirties. I'll never forget his warm, fierce handclasp—the handshake he had, not for the receiving line, but for his friends. The last time I shook hands with him—last September—I was shocked to find that his hand felt soft and sort of flabby, like the hand of an old man. How much better for him to go quickly this way. He would have so bitterly resented the kind of disintegration that comes with old age. Darling; sometimes I may get straightened out the mixed personal and shall I say public feelings I have about you and your family! I'm trusting you implicitly in not going to Washington or to H.P. just now. After all, I do know how you feel about state funerals and all that sort of thing. I shall go into New York next Thursday afternoon and have my blood sugar Friday morning. I'll see the doctor Saturday morning and from then on—and as long as we both shall live—I shall be yours to command.

Dear one, I love you will all my heart—H

page 128:

HARRY TRUMAN TO BESS TRUMAN

Dear Bess:

Just two months ago today, I was a reasonably happy and contented Vice-President. Maybe you can remember that far back too. But things have changed so much it hardly seems real.

I sit here in this old house and work on foreign affairs, read reports, and work on speeches—all the while listening to the ghosts walk up and down the hallway and even right here in the study. The floors pop and the drapes move back and forth—I can just imagine old Andy and Teddy having an argument over Franklin. Or James Buchanan and Franklin Pierce deciding which was more useless to the country. And when Millar Filmore and Chester Arthur join in for place and show the din is almost unbearable. But I still get some work done.

Hope the weather lets up and you will be able to do some work on the house. The Gibson boy should have been taken care of long ago. I'll see what's happened. I'm not able to do as many things for my friends as I did when I was just a dirty organization Democrat and a County Judge.

Guess you and Helen will have a grand time. Hope you do. We are working on Dr. Wallace. Glad everybody was in his right mind at the family party. Undoubtedly they were walking the straight and narrow for your mother. But I'm sure you had a nice time anyway.

That address mixed up is causing me some embarrassment (if that's the way you spell that {illegible} word.) I addressed a letter to you at 4701 Conn. Ave. Independence, Mo., and another one 219 North Delaware, Washington, D.C. Now it seems I sent one to the {illegible}. The boys in the House here did not catch that one but they did the other two. I'll have {illegible} attend to the choices you suggest. I haven't seen her but twice since you left. She comes in after I go over to the office, usually goes out to lunch and doesn't come back until I am gone again and then goes home before I get over here.

Had Charlie Ross & Rosenman to lunch yesterday. We worked on my San Francisco speech. That date is postponed until next week now on account of the slow wind up and Gen. Eisenhower's visit.

Write me when you can—I hope every day. Lots of love

page 146:

LADY BIRD JOHNSON TO LYNDON JOHNSON

Beloved,

You are as brave a man as Harry Truman—or FDR—or Lincoln. You can go on to find some peace, some achievement amidst all the pain. You have been strong, patient, determined beyond any words of mine to express. I honor you for it. So does most of the country.

To step out now could be wrong for your country, and I can see nothing but a lonely waste land for your future. Your friends would be frozen in embarrassed silence and your enemies jeering.

I am not afraid of Time or lies or losing money on defeat. In the final analysis, I can't carry any of the burdens you talked of—so I know its only your choice. But I know you are as brave as any of the thirty-five.

I love you always.

page 170:

VICTORIA TIMMONS SCHMITT TO NANCY REAGAN

July 30, 1981
Dear Mrs. Reagan,
I have never in my life written a letter to a celebrity, not even to a teenage singing idol, but I have felt compelled to communicate my admiration of your portrayal of our First Lady to you personally.

During the election campaign of your husband, through the inauguration you have displayed an elegance and charm that is uplifting to this wife and mother. I was especially proud of your representation of our country at the Royal Wedding. You displayed such good taste in your wardrobe, you looked absolutely stunning. You also made an excellent addition to the beauty of the occasion.

My husband and I strongly support the programs your husband and you are trying to put through for the restoration of the United States. We feel Mr. Reagan is the most capable man we have had as President in decades. We wish him our very best and hope he is feeling fully recovered from the shooting.

I know you receive thousands of letters every week and probably won't read this personally, but I do hope your assistants will give you the message I have sent.

Before I close I know you have received criticism on your ideas of the role of a women, wife and mother in our society. But I for one totally agree with you. I have a wonderful husband who works very hard as a sales manager for an oil storage tank company and as a vice-president of his own oil service company, and I have a wonderful beautiful 16 month old baby boy. And I know that if I don't give my full support to my husband and son that everyone's life would be very unhappy, especially mine. So what ever public grumbling you hear, remember always that there are those of us in this country who hold your ideas in very high esteem. We truly appreciate your unwavering stand on your convictions.

Again, thank you for being a lovely and admirable First Lady. Please give my regards to our President. God bless and keep you both in His care. Our prayers are with you.

∽

page 172:
Ronald Reagan to Nancy Reagan

The White House
Washington
Dec. 25 1981

Dear Mrs. R.
I still don't feel right about you opening an envelope instead of a gift package.

There are several much beloved women in my life and on Christmas I should be giving them gold, precious stones, perfume, furs and lace. I know that even the best of these would still fall far short of expressing how much these several women mean to me and how empty my life would be without them.

There is of course my "First Lady." She brings so much grace and charm to whatever she does that even stuffy formal functions sparkle and turn unto fun times. Everything is done with class. All I have to do is wash up and show up.

There is another woman in my life who does things I don't always get to see but I hear about them and sometimes see photos of her doing them. She takes an abandoned child in her arms on a hospital visit. The look on her face only the Madonna could match. The look on the child's face is one of adoration. I know because I adore her too.

She bends over a wheelchair or a bed to touch an elderly invalid with tenderness and compassion just as she fills my life with warmth and love.

There is another gal I love who is a nest builder. If she were stuck three days in a hotel room she'd manage to make it home sweet home. She moves things around—looks at it—straightens this and that and you wonder why it wasn't that way in the first place.

I'm also crazy about the girl who goes to the ranch with me. If we were tidying up the woods she's a {illegible} power house at pushing over dead trees. She's a wonderful person to sit by the fire with, or to ride with or just to be with when the sun goes down or the stars come out. If she ever stopped going to the ranch, I'd stop too because I'd see her in every beauty spot there is and I couldn't stand that.

Then there is a sentimental lady I love whose eyes fill up so easily. On the other hand she loves to laugh and her laugh is like tinkling bells and feel good all over even if I tell a joke she's heard before.

Fortunately all these women in my life are you—fortunately for me that is, for there could be no life for me without you. Browning asked; "How do I love thee—let me count the ways?" For me there is no way to count. I love the whole gang of you—Mommie, first lady, the sentimental you, the fun you and the {illegible} power house you.

And oh yes, one other very special you—the little girl who takes a "nana" to bed in case she gets hungry in the night. I couldn't & don't sleep well if she isn't there—so please always be there.

Merry Christmas you all—with all my love.
Lucky me.

About the Contributors

DWIGHT YOUNG has been actively involved in historic preservation for almost 30 years. He joined the staff of the National Trust for Historic Preservation in 1977 and moved to Trust headquarters in Washington in 1992. He is the author of *Alternatives to Sprawl*, *Saving America's Treasures*, and *Dear Mr. President: Letters to the Oval Office from the Files of the National Archives*, the model for *Dear First Lady*. Young is perhaps best known as author of the "Back Page" feature in *Preservation* magazine. In 2003, the National Trust published a collection of these essays titled *Road Trips Through History*.

MARGARET JOHNSON is a researcher and editor based in Washington, D.C. She was a 2006 Emmy Award nominee for Outstanding Achievement in Research for the PBS documentary *American Experience: Victory in the Pacific*. Her books include *Dear Mr. President: Letters to the Oval Office from the Files of the National Archives*, *An American Idea: The Making of the National Parks*, *Songcatchers*, and *Battlegrounds: Geography and the History of Warfare*. *Dear First Lady* is her fifth book for National Geographic.

HELEN THOMAS, frequently referred to as "First Lady of the Press," is the former White House bureau chief for United Press International. For 57 years, she served as White House correspondent, covering every President since John F. Kennedy. In 2000, Thomas left her post at UPI and joined Hearst Newspapers as a syndicated columnist. She is the author of *Dateline: White House*; *Front Row at the White House*, a memoir; and *Thanks for the Memories, Mr. President*. Her latest book, *Watchdogs of Democracy?* about how professional journalism has changed, was published in June 2006.

Acknowledgments

The authors and project editor wish to thank the following individuals who assisted substantially in the editorial development of this book.

LIBRARY OF CONGRESS
Lia Apodaca, Frederick Augustyn, Barbara Bair, Jennifer Brathovde, Kimberli Curry, Jeffrey Flannery, Gerard Gawalt, John Haynes, James Hutson, Joseph Jackson, Patrick Kerwin, Bruce Kirby, and John Sellers

NATIONAL ARCHIVES
AND RECORDS ADMINISTRATION
Christina Hardman, Michael Hussey, Trevor Plante, and James Zeender

PRESIDENTIAL LIBRARIES
Claudia Anderson, Laurie Austin, Steve Branch, Tom Branigar, Bonnie Burlbaw, Debbie Carter, Brooke Clement, Barbara Cline, Bridget Crowley, Stacy Davis, Jim Detlefsen, Mike Duggan, Laura Eggert, Allan Goodrich, Maryrose Grossman, Kenneth Hafeli, David Haight, Margaret Harman, Kelly Hendren, John Keller, Sharon Kelly, Tammy Kelly, Michelle Kopfer, Jim Leyerzapf, Youlanda Logan, Tom McNaught, Mary Anne McSweeney, Steve Plotkin, Wren Powell, John Powers, Mark Renovitch, Sam Rushay, Neena Sachdeva, Sara Saunders, Matthew Schaeffer, Cate Sewell, Randy Sowell, and Alycia Vivona

Note: The Presidential Library system is composed of 12 Presidential Libraries. These facilities are overseen by the Office of Presidential Libraries in the National Archives and Records Administration.

THE WHITE HOUSE
Office of First Lady Laura Bush

AND
Antonia Coffman, *The Simpsons*; William Copeley and Peter Wallner, *New Hampshire Historical Society*; Christina Gehring, *Foundation for the National Archives*; Lisa Lytton, *Paraculture, Inc.*; and Deborah Thawley.

LETTER CITATIONS

LIBRARY OF CONGRESS MANUSCRIPT DIVISION
Washington, D.C.

Page 20: George Washington Papers, Series 4; Letter, John Trumbull to Martha Washington, October 7, 1796

Page 22: George Washington Papers, Series 4; Letter, A. St. Mary to Martha Washington, December 17, 1796

Page 28: Thomas Jefferson Papers, Series 1; Letter, Thomas Jefferson to Abigail Adams, June 13, 1804

Page 30: Dolley Madison Papers, Container 1; Letter, Dolley Madison to Anna Cutts, August 23, 1814

Page 36: James Buchanan and Harriet Lane Johnston Papers, Series 2, Box 2; Letter, Wingematub to Harriet Lane, February 4, 1858

Page 38: Abraham Lincoln Papers, Series 3, Number 978; Letter, Helen M. Rauschnabel to Mary Todd Lincoln, May 7, 1861

Page 40: Abraham Lincoln Papers, Series 1, Number 4238; Letter, Mary Todd Lincoln to Abraham Lincoln, November 3, 1862

Page 42: Abraham Lincoln Papers; Letter, Abraham Lincoln to Mary Todd Lincoln, August 8, 1863

Page 46: Abraham Lincoln Papers, Series 3, Number 43634; Letter, Queen Victoria to Mary Todd Lincoln, April 29, 1865

Page 48: Andrew Johnson Papers, Series 1; Letter, Jonathan French to Eliza Johnson, May 19, 1868

Page 50: Ulysses S. Grant Papers, Series 1A; Notes, Julia Grant to Ulysses S. Grant, May 22, 1875

Page 52: James Garfield Papers, Series 4, V 133/480; Letter, Mrs. E. C. Sloan to Lucretia Garfield, March 8, 1881

Page 54: James Garfield Papers, Series 4, V 140/254; Letter, Mrs. M. A. McMaster to Lucretia Garfield, May 11, 1881

Page 56 up: James Garfield Papers, Series 4; Telegram, Moses Hunt to Lucretia Garfield, August 19, 1881

Page 56 low: James Garfield Papers, Series 6B, V003/192; Telegram, A. F. Rockwell to Lucretia Garfield, July 2, 1881

Page 58: Benjamin Harrison Papers, Series 2; Letter, Howard Carter to Caroline Harrison, October 1892

Page 60: Grover Cleveland Papers, Series 3; Letter, Mrs. G. H. Cleveland to Frances Cleveland, May 21, 1887

Page 62: Grover Cleveland Papers, Series 3; Letter, Sally Walker Boor to Frances Cleveland, September 14, 1893

Page 64: Grover Cleveland Papers, Series 3; Letter, Frances Cleveland to H. T. Thurber, July 11, 1894

Page 66: William McKinley Papers, Series 3; Letter, Mrs. Susan Wolfskill to Ida McKinley, May 16, 1901

Page 68: William McKinley Papers, Series 11; Cards, sympathy expressions to Ida McKinley, September-December 1901

Page 69: William McKinley Papers, Series 3; Invitation, Pan American Exposition to Ida McKinley, May 20, 1901

Page 70: Theodore Roosevelt Papers, Series 2; Carbon, Edith Roosevelt to Charles F. McKim, September 18, 1902

Page 72: Kermit Roosevelt Papers, Box 9, Edith Roosevelt file; Letter, Kermit Roosevelt to Edith Roosevelt, April 26, 1903

Page 74: Theodore Roosevelt Papers, Series 1; Letter, Whitelaw Reid to Edith Roosevelt, June 1, 1906

Page 76: William Howard Taft Papers, Series 3; Letter, Helen Taft to William Howard Taft, July 1909

Page 78: William Howard Taft Papers, Series 5, Case File 3316; Letter, Mrs. Pincus Schein to Helen Taft, March 9, 1910

Page 80: William Howard Taft Papers, Series 27, Part A Box 1 Folder 35; Draft letter, Helen Taft to Madame Yukio Ozaki, undated

Page 82: Woodrow Wilson Papers, Series 4, CF 4A25; Letter, A Temperate Printer to Ellen Wilson, April 17, 1913

Page 84: Woodrow Wilson Papers, Series 4, CF 84; Letter, Edith E. Wood to Ellen Wilson, September 25, 1913

Page 86 up: Woodrow Wilson Papers, Series 20, Container 2, Folder 5, Edith Bolling (Galt) Wilson, 1921; Letter, Woodrow Wilson to Edith Wilson, 1921

Page 86 low: Wilson Papers, Series 20, Container 2, Edith Bolling (Galt) Wilson, Family Correspondence, 1915, Oct-Dec; Card, Woodrow Wilson to Edith Wilson, December 18, 1915

Page 88: Woodrow Wilson Papers, Series 9, Vol 2, p. 21, Scrapbook; Letters, Franklin K. Lane to Edith Wilson, May Gonzalez to Franklin K. Lane, April 10, 1917

Page 90: Woodrow Wilson Papers, Series 2; Letter, Joseph Tumulty to Edith Wilson, December 18, 1919

Page 92: Evalyn Walsh McLean Collection, Box 6, Folder: Warren G. Harding; Letter, Florence Harding to Evalyn Walsh McLean, August 25, 1923

NATIONAL ARCHIVES AND RECORDS ADMINISTRATION
Washington, D.C.

Page 45: Telegram, Abraham Lincoln to Mary Todd Lincoln, April 28, 1864; Telegrams Sent and Received by the War Department Central Telegraph Office, Entry 34; Records of the Office of the Secretary of War, RG 107

Page 94: Letter, Syngman Rhee to Grace Coolidge, July 8, 1924; Decimal File Number 811.0011; Box 7343, Central Decimal Files, 1910-1929, Records of the Department of State, RG 59

HERBERT HOOVER PRESIDENTIAL LIBRARY AND MUSEUM
West Branch, IA

Page 96: Letter, The Women's League of Miami, Florida, to Lou Hoover, June 18, 1929; Lou Hoover Papers, Subject Files, DePriest Incident, Box 52

Page 99: Letter, A. E. Bruce to Lou Hoover, June 16, 1929; Lou Hoover Papers, Subject Files, DePriest Incident, Box 51

Page 100: Letters, Students to Lou Hoover, 1929, n.d., Lou Hoover Papers, Subject file, Rapidan Camp, President's School, Children's Letters, Box 77

Page 102: Letter, Pearl N. Schmitt to Lou Hoover, November 15, 1932; Lou Hoover Papers, Subject Files, Depression, Box 14

Page 106: Letter, Lou Hoover to Grace Coolidge, January 23, 1933; Lou Hoover Papers, Correspondence 1929-33, Coolidge, Grace

FRANKLIN D. ROOSEVELT PRESIDENTIAL LIBRARY AND MUSEUM
Hyde Park, NY

Page 108: Memo, Franklin D. Roosevelt to Eleanor Roosevelt, March 17, 1933, Roosevelt Family Papers Donated by the

Children, Series II, Correspondence, Franklin Roosevelt to Eleanor Roosevelt and Children

Page 110: Letter, Lorena Hickok to Eleanor Roosevelt, November 28, 1933, Lorena Hickok Papers

Page 112: Letter, Clara Leonard to Eleanor Roosevelt, December 14, 1934, Eleanor Roosevelt Papers, White House Correspondence, Series 150.1, Material Assistance Requested

Page 114: Letter, Mrs. H. Goldfarb to Eleanor Roosevelt, May 8, 1935, Eleanor Roosevelt Papers, White House Correspondence, Series 70, Correspondence with Government Departments

Page 116: Carbon, Eleanor Roosevelt to Mrs. Henry M. Robert, Jr., Daughters of the American Revolution, February 26, 1939, Eleanor Roosevelt Papers, White House Correspondence, Series 100, Personal Letters

Page 118: Letter, Pearl S. Buck to Eleanor Roosevelt, May 22, 1942, Eleanor Roosevelt Papers, White House Correspondence, Series 100, Personal Letter; *Published with permission of Pearl S. Buck Family Trust*

Page 120-121: Letter, Pvt. Clifton Searles to Eleanor Roosevelt, January 11, 1942 [sic], with enclosure, Eleanor Roosevelt Papers, White House Correspondence, Series 100.1, Letters from Servicemen [note: letter dated 1942 but it was actually 1943] *Published with permission of Mrs. Lorraine E. Searles and daughters Daphine, DeVora & Julie*

Page 123: Letter, Eleanor Roosevelt to Pvt. Clifton Searles, January 23, 1943, Eleanor Roosevelt Papers, White House Correspondence, Series 100.1, Letters from Servicemen

Page 124 up: Post card, Jeff Davis to Eleanor Roosevelt, June 23, 1943, White House Correspondence Files, Series 70, Correspondence with Government Departments, Race Riots

Page 124 low: Post card, Francis Jackson to Eleanor Roosevelt, June 24, 1943, White House Correspondence Files, Series 70, Correspondence with Government Departments, Race Riots

Page 126: Letter, Lorena Hickok to Eleanor Roosevelt, April 13, 1945, Lorena Hickok Papers

HARRY S. TRUMAN PRESIDENTIAL LIBRARY AND MUSEUM
Independence, MO

Page 128: Letter, Harry Truman to Bess Truman, June 12, 1945; Correspondence from Harry S. Truman to Bess Wallace Truman, Family Correspondence File, Papers Pertaining to Family, Business and Personal Affairs, Harry S. Truman Papers

DWIGHT D. EISENHOWER PRESIDENTIAL LIBRARY AND MUSEUM
Abilene, KS

Page 130-131: Letter and Drawings, Elizabeth Arden to Mamie Eisenhower, February 20, 1953; White House Series, MDE Papers, Box 2; Arden, Elizabeth (only)

Page 132: Telegram, Sophie Rosenberg to Mrs. Dwight D. Eisenhower, June 16, 1953; Eisenhower Records as President, White House Central Files, Alphabetical Index, Box 2672; Rosenbergs, The (Julius and Ethel) (1)

Page 134: Cards, Julie and Patricia Nixon to Mrs. Eisenhower, November 17, 1954; White House Series, MDE Papers, Box 32; Nixon File

JOHN F. KENNEDY PRESIDENTIAL LIBRARY AND MUSEUM
Boston, MA

Page 136: Letter, Michele Timmons to Mrs. Kennedy, February 19, 1962, White House Social Files, Box 904, Folder: Trip (India)–T. *Published with permission of Michele Timmons Hanna*

Pages 138 and 141: Letter from Arthur Schlesinger, Jr. to Jacqueline Kennedy, July 17, 1962, Arthur M. Schlesinger, Jr. Papers (#206), Series 2, Correspondence, 1961-1965, Box: P-35, Folder: Kennedy, J-Khol

LYNDON B. JOHNSON PRESIDENTIAL LIBRARY AND MUSEUM
Austin, TX

Page 6: Letter, Helen Thomas to Mrs. Johnson, October 28, 1965, White House Social Files, Alphabetical File, Box 1962, Thomas–H. *Published with permission of Helen Thomas*

Page 144: Thermofax of letter, Lyndon Johnson to Jacqueline Kennedy, December 1, 1963, White House Famous Names File, Box 6, Folder: Kennedy, Mrs. John F. 1963

Page 146: Letter, Lady Bird Johnson to President Johnson, August 1964; Personal Papers of Mrs. Johnson, Box 3, Folder: August 1964, President's Decision to run in 1964

Page 148: Letter, Jacque McKone to Mrs. Johnson, October 4, 1964, White House Social Files, Alpha, Box 1653, Folder: Photograph (sent) McKay; *Published with permission of Jackie McKone*

Page 150: Letter, Merrick School Mothers Club to Mrs. Johnson, March 10, 1965, White House Social Files, Alpha. Folder: Beautification–Mercer

Page 153: Letter, Terry Fiskin to Mrs. Johnson, April 5, 1965, White House Social Files, Alpha, Box 83, Folder: Beautification–Austin. *Published with permission of the Auto Dismantlers Association of Southern California*

Page 154: Letter, Gena Geedy to Mrs. Johnson, August 11, 1967, White House Social Files, Alpha, Box 1705, Folder: Project Head Start–G. *Published with permission of Mrs. Virginia L. Winitsky*

Page 156: Bessie Mae Smith to Mrs. Johnson, March 13, 1968, White House Social Files, Alpha, Box 1614, Folder: Pease

RICHARD M. NIXON PRESIDENTIAL LIBRARY AND MUSEUM
Yorba Linda, CA

Page 158: Letter, Pat Nixon to Mrs. Alicia Marrero, August 3, 1974: White House Central Files, Staff and Member Office Files, Gwendolyn B. King: Form Responses, Box 8, Folder: Friendship/Support

GERALD R. FORD PRESIDENTIAL LIBRARY AND MUSEUM
Ann Arbor, MI

Page 160: Letter, Mrs. Ernie Ford to Betty Ford, September 1974, White House Office Files, Subject File, 1974-77; Box 13, Folder: FL 4. *Published with permission of Jeffery Buckner Ford*

Page 162: Letter, Maria von Trapp to Betty Ford, August 12, 1975, Vertical File; Ford, Betty, 1918- ; Letters to

Page 164: Letter, Richard Nixon to Betty Ford, May 23, 1975, Vertical File, Ford Betty, 1918- ; Letters to

Page 166: Letter, Roxie Lee McCarty to Betty Ford, June 28, 1976, White House Social Files, Subject File 1974-77, Box 30, Folder: FL 15-17/ST 11-15

JIMMY CARTER PRESIDENTIAL LIBRARY AND MUSEUM
Atlanta, GA

Page 168: Memo, Patrick H. Caddell to Rosalynn Carter, July 30, 1977, Jody Powell's Files, Box 42, Folder: Memorandum: First Lady's Staff 2/7/77–10/14/77 [CF O/A 55]

RONALD REAGAN PRESIDENTIAL LIBRARY AND MUSEUM
Simi Valley, CA

Page 170: Letter, Victoria Timmons Schmitt to Nancy Reagan, July 30, 1981, ID#035534, PP005-01, White House Office of Records Management: Subject File. *Published with permission of Victoria T. Carruthers*

Page 172: Letter, Ronald Reagan to Nancy Reagan, December 25, 1981, folder "Christmas Letters (2)," Box 5, Nancy Davis Reagan Papers. *From "I Love You, Ronnie" by Nancy Reagan, © 2000 by Ronald Reagan Presidential Foundation. Used by permission of Random House, Inc.*

Page 175: Note, Ronald Reagan to Nancy Reagan, March 4, 1983, Folder "Anniversary (March 4) Letters (2)" Box 2, Nancy Davis Reagan Papers. *From "I Love You, Ronnie" by Nancy Reagan, © 2000 by Ronald Reagan Presidential Foundation. Used by permission of Random House, Inc.*

Page 176: Letter, Margaret M. Shozda to Nancy Reagan, March 19, 1982, ID#074924, PPOO5-01, White House Office of Records Management: Subject File. *Published with permission of Margaret Schozda*

GEORGE BUSH PRESIDENTIAL LIBRARY AND MUSEUM
College Station, TX

Page 178: Letter, Tasha to Millie Bush, October 17, 1989, Bush Presidential Records, First Lady's Office of Correspondence, Joan Decain Files, Folder "Millie Mail & Robo Response; Mrs. Bush & Joan Decain Letters [7]". *Published with permission of Tasha (Sangston) Davis*

Page 180: Letter, [Name Redacted] to Mrs. George Bush, January 29, 1990, Bush Presidential Records, White House Office of Records Management, Subject File, TR057, Case Number 126193, Unscanned

Page 182: Letter, Marge Simpson to Mrs. Barbara Bush, September 28, 1990, Bush Presidential Records, White House Office of Records Management Subject File, PP005-01, Case Number 190753. *Published with permission of The Simpsons and Twentieth Century Fox Film Corporation*

WILLIAM J. CLINTON PRESIDENTIAL LIBRARY AND MUSEUM
Little Rock, AR

Page 184: Letter, Dalai Lama to Hillary Clinton, October 30, 1995, Hillary Rodham Clinton Personal Materials, Installed Exhibit Material

Page 186: Letter, Esther "Eppie" Lederer to Hillary Rodham Clinton, December 5, 1998, Hillary Rodham Clinton Personal Materials, Installed Exhibit Material. *Published with permission of Margo Howard Trust*

THE WHITE HOUSE
Washington, D.C.

Page 188: Letter, First Lady Laura Bush to Elementary School Students, September 12, 2001: White House Office of Records Management, Subject File, ID# 492577, PP005-01, p. 111.

Page 190: Letter, Deborah Butryn to First Lady Laura Bush, March 12, 2003: White House Office of Records Management, Subject File, ID# 544919, PP005-01. *Published with permission of Deborah Butryn*

MASSACHUSETTS HISTORICAL SOCIETY
Boston, MA

Page 26: Adams Family Papers; Letter, John Adams to Abigail Adams, November 2, 1800. *Courtesy of the Massachusetts Historical Society*

NEW HAMPSHIRE HISTORICAL SOCIETY
Concord, NH

Page 32: Letter, A.D. Dearborn and N.D. Dearborn to Jane Pierce, January 4, 1853

Page 35: Letter, Jane Pierce to Benny Pierce, January 1853

Page 142: Letter, Bernard Boutin to Jacqueline Kennedy, April 9, 1963

༜

ILLUSTRATIONS CREDITS

Dear First Lady

Dwight Young and Margaret Johnson

PUBLISHED BY THE NATIONAL GEOGRAPHIC SOCIETY

John M. Fahey, Jr., *President and Chief Executive Officer*

Gilbert M. Grosvenor, *Chairman of the Board*

Tim T. Kelly, *President, Global Media Group*

John Q. Griffin, *Executive Vice President;*
    President, Publishing

Nina D. Hoffman, *Executive Vice President;*
    President, Book Publishing Group

PREPARED BY THE BOOK DIVISION

Barbara Brownell Grogan, *Vice President and*
    Editor in Chief

Marianne R. Koszorus, *Director of Design*

Susan Tyler Hitchcock, *Senior Editor*

R. Gary Colbert, *Production Director*

Jennifer A. Thornton, *Managing Editor*

Meredith C. Wilcox, *Administrative Director, Illustrations*

STAFF FOR THIS BOOK

Garrett W. Brown, *Editor*

Judith Klein, *Copy Editor*

Margaret Johnson, *Photo Editor and Researcher*

Melissa Farris, *Art Director*

Cameron Zotter, *Designer*

Marshall Kiker, *Illustrations Specialist*

Richard S. Wain, *Production Manager*

MANUFACTURING AND QUALITY MANAGEMENT

Christopher A. Liedel, *Chief Financial Officer*

Phillip L. Schlosser, *Vice President*

Chris Brown, *Technical Director*

Nicole Elliott, *Manager*

Rachel Faulise, *Manager*

The National Geographic Society is one of the world's largest nonprofit scientific and educational organizations. Founded in 1888 to "increase and diffuse geographic knowledge," the Society works to inspire people to care about the planet. It reaches more than 325 million people worldwide each month through its official journal, *National Geographic,* and other magazines; National Geographic Channel; television documentaries; music; radio; films; books; DVDs; maps; exhibitions; school publishing programs; interactive media; and merchandise. National Geographic has funded more than 9,000 scientific research, conservation and exploration projects and supports an education program combating geographic illiteracy.

For more information, please call 1-800-NGS LINE (647-5463) or write to the following address:

National Geographic Society
1145 17th Street N.W.
Washington, D.C. 20036-4688 U.S.A.

Visit us online at www.nationalgeographic.com

For information about special discounts for bulk purchases, please contact National Geographic Books Special Sales: ngspecsales@ngs.org

For rights or permissions inquiries, please contact National Geographic Books Subsidiary Rights: ngbookrights@ngs.org

This edition published in 2009

ISBN 978-1-4262-0589-7
ISBN 978-1-4262-0590-3 (deluxe edition)

The original hardcover edition is cataloged by the Library of Congress as follows:

Dear First Lady : letters to the White House / [compiled and edited] by Dwight Young and Margaret Johnson ; foreword by Helen Thomas.
    p. cm.
  ISBN 978-1-4262-0087-8 (hardcover : alk. paper)
  1. Presidents' spouses--United States--Correspondence. 2. American letters. I. Young, Dwight. II. Johnson, Margaret, 1949 Mar. 15-
E176.2.D43 2008
973.09'9--dc22

                       2007045186

Printed in U.S.A.

09/RRDW/1